A HANDBOOK
EXPER
IN CHILD

A HANDBOOK FOR EXPERT WITNESSES IN CHILDREN ACT CASES

Second Edition

Nicholas Wall

A Lord Justice of Appeal

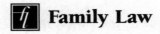 **Family Law**

Published by Family Law

A publishing imprint of
Jordan Publishing Limited
21 St Thomas Street
Bristol BS1 6JS

© Jordan Publishing Limited 2007

British Library Cataloguing-in-Publication Data

A catalogue record for this book is available from the British Library

ISBN 978 1 84661 034 9

Typeset by Etica Press Ltd, Malvern, Worcs WR14 1ET
Printed and bound in Great Britain by Antony Rowe Ltd, Chippenham, Wilts

FOREWORD

Since Lord Justice Wall (then Mr Justice Wall) published the first edition of this excellent Handbook in 2000, the work of the family courts has come increasingly under the public gaze. Several high-profile cases have increased awareness of the complexity of the issues which confront family judges and magistrates, who are responsible for making some of the most important, difficult and long lasting decisions of any jurisdiction. Lord Justice Wall has himself been involved in illuminating those issues in a number of appellate judgments.

In October 2006, the Chief Medical Officer, in his report entitled 'Bearing Good Witness' noted the increasing volume of cases and a perceived trend towards the greater use of, and demand for, experts. His report made clear that many doctors continue to regard the courtroom as an unfamiliar and hostile environment and remain both reluctant and anxious about giving evidence in family cases relating to children.

This second edition of the Handbook is particularly welcome, tackling head-on, as it does, the major challenges facing any expert instructed to provide an opinion to assist the court in arriving at the appropriate decision.

The guidance provided is wise, detailed and practical. Its content is a model of orderly presentation, dealing in logical order with all the questions which need to be answered in clear and reassuring terms. It begins with an explanation of the three cardinal principles governing family proceedings and moves to close examination of the processes of taking instructions, report writing and court attendance. There is welcome recognition that courts and lawyers have not always understood the role of different experts or provided adequate instruction to them. This has been addressed in Appendix C to the present Public Law Protocol (PLP) which is set out and discussed in Chapter 26. The reader can be assured that, when the author states that none of the guidance in the handbook is in any way inconsistent with the currently proposed changes to the PLP, he speaks with authority.

Because of the importance of the case of *Meadow v GMC*,[1] the Handbook includes a detailed exposition of its content. Lord Justice Wall is clear that the message to be learned from this case is that, if the work of the expert is conscientiously undertaken and the evidence given is honest, fair and well-reasoned, then provided the expert is giving evidence within his area of expertise, he or she has nothing to fear, and much to gain, from participating in family proceedings as an expert witness.

While the Handbook is addressed to medical experts, this revised edition should be required reading for all practitioners concerned with the instruction of such experts and the evaluation and examination of their reports. Indeed, I commend it to every professional who works with children in the family justice system as a slim but indispensable addition to their library.

Mark Potter.

Sir Mark Potter

President of the Family Division
Head of Family Justice

---

[1]   [2006] EWCA Civ 1390.

FOREWORD

The Royal College of Paediatrics and Child Health welcomes the second edition of the Experts Handbook. Paediatricians recognise their duty to the courts in child protection cases but, in many instances, have found this a challenging experience. This excellent and useful Handbook promotes good practice by providing practical advice and guidance, and encouraging doctors and other health professionals to take on this work for the benefit of children and young people. Raising standards and displaying good practice will help professionals and families alike, and the production of the second edition of the Experts Handbook demonstrates how much its contribution to this difficult area has been appreciated. I would encourage all paediatricians to read and learn from this book, as I believe they will benefit greatly from it.

Patricia Hamilton

President
Royal College of Paediatrics and Child Health

INTRODUCTION TO THE SECOND EDITION

This Handbook has been out of print for some time and the publishers have invited me to produce a second edition.

The three principal purposes for which this Handbook was written are set out in the first paragraph of the introduction to the first edition, which is reprinted at pages xiii to xv below. Those three purposes are unchanged, although the emphasis has, I think, shifted. In the events which have occurred since the first edition was produced in 2000, I now regard this book as principally addressing the second of the purposes I identified in 2000, namely that of encouraging doctors and mental health professionals who have expertise in relation to children to undertake work in Children Act proceedings as expert witnesses.

Although I no longer sit at first instance, I continue to be told that doctors regard the courtroom as a hostile environment, and that they remain anxious about giving expert evidence in family cases relating to children. Of course, the courtroom is not your usual working environment, as it is for the lawyers. I recognise that it can be a lonely and testing place. However, the importance of your contribution to the lives of the children and families with whom the Family Justice System deals cannot be overemphasised or stated too often.

There is, in my view, no more important issue in family justice than child protection. Care proceedings are at the limit of the court's powers and frequently engage the most fundamental questions. They determine children's lives. On the one hand, returning an abused child to abusive parents is, sometimes, quite literally a matter of life and death: on the other, parents who lose their children frequently talk of being given 'a life sentence'. The stakes simply could not be higher and you should not underestimate either the importance of the work or the value of your contribution towards it.

As the introduction to the first edition of this work explained, and as I now repeat, the object of this Handbook is to dispel misunderstandings and to instil in you the confidence which will enable you to make your vital contribution to the cause of forensic child protection. It is a principal theme of the Handbook (and in my view the principal lesson to be learned from the case of *Meadow v GMC*, to which the first chapter of this edition is devoted) that if your work is conscientiously undertaken, your report and oral evidence honest, fair and well-reasoned, and provided that you have worked within the area of your expertise, you have nothing to fear, and much to gain from participating in family proceedings as an expert witness.

There is rarely an ideal time to publish a new edition of a book on any aspect of family law. The reason for this is self-evident. Family Law is constantly evolving and developing. Developments in its approach and its thinking – more perhaps than in any other branch of the law, reflect – and sometimes anticipate – social and political change.

Self-evidently, therefore, a great deal has happened in the field of expert evidence since this Handbook was published in 2000, and the process of change is ongoing. Much of what has happened since 2000 has been dispiriting. The series of high profile criminal cases, notably *R v Cannings* and *R v Clark*, have done much to dent public confidence in the value of expert evidence. The fear of being reported to your professional body – as in the case of *Meadow v GMC* – has added to doctors' reluctance to proffer themselves as expert witnesses in proceedings relating to children. Chapter 1 of the Handbook, which is devoted to that case, attempts to dispel that fear.

So the message of the Handbook remains the same. Child protection continues to be, and will always be, a matter of the utmost importance. The contribution you make to the forensic process in cases involving children is enormous, and invaluable. This Handbook recognises all the disincentives, but urges you to participate. As the introduction to the first edition makes clear, and as I have already stated, the wish to combat your reluctance to become engaged in forensic child protection work was one of three catalysts for the first edition of the Handbook, and now takes centre stage.

Not everything which has happened in the last seven years has been negative. On the positive side has been the development of the Protocol for Judicial Case Management in Public Law Children Act Cases (The Protocol) and the creation of the Family Justice Council (the FJC), to which Chapters 26 and 27 respectively are devoted.

As with other aspects of family law, the process of change in the field of expert evidence is ongoing. In particular, work is currently in progress on what is to be called 'the Public Law Outline' and a new body of rules for all family proceedings, to be known as the Family Procedure Rules. These developments need not concern you, although the new rules will contain a code for the provision of expert evidence, the essence of which is to be found in the proposed draft Practice Direction printed as Appendix 11. This will replace Appendix C of the Protocol, set out in Chapter 26. You may take it, however, that none of the proposed changes is likely to alter or contradict anything said in this Handbook.

On a closely related topic, the question of your fees for reporting and giving evidence in proceedings under the Children Act remains a matter of ongoing debate between the profession and the Legal Services Commission.

Despite these unresolved issues, two particular events have – in my mind at least – expedited the republication and updating of the Handbook. The first, of course, is the decision of the Court of Appeal in *Meadow v GMC* to which I have already referred. The second is the report of the Chief Medical Officer, Sir Liam Donaldson *Bearing Good Witness – Proposals for Reforming the Delivery of Medical Expert Evidence in Family Law Cases.*

Opinions differ on the CMO's report. Some welcome it as an innovative attempt to resolve the current shortage of expert witnesses and to import a forensic element into medical training and into the contracts of doctors engaged in the field of child protection. Others dismiss it as both impractical and counterproductive and, if implemented, likely at best to dilute, and at worst to eradicate the independence required for truly expert advice.

This Handbook is not the place in which to engage in that debate. I have, moreover, not addressed the report in the body of the text for one very simple reason. Even assuming that the CMO's proposals were to be accepted by the government, the report is unlikely to be implemented during the life-time of this edition of the Handbook. It is principally for this reason that there are only passing references to it in the text. I am, however, confident that nothing in the report contradicts anything in the Handbook.

The Handbook retains the format of the first edition. The text remains addressed to you in the second person plural. There are new chapters on a number of developments in the field since 2000, notably the Protocol (Chapter 26), the creation and activities of the FJC (Chapter 27) and the British and Irish Legal Information Institute (BAILII – Chapter 36). I have also taken the opportunity to add material on a number of issues of practice which have surfaced since the first edition of the Handbook, notably the proper reaction of the expert who is put under pressure to take a particular course (an expanded Chapter 11); the undesirability of accepting anonymised instructions (Chapter 31); and the impact of the European Convention on Human Rights and the Human Rights Act 1998 (implemented in October 2000) (Chapter 28). Generally speaking, Chapters 1, and 26 to 35 contain fresh material: Chapters 2 to 25 have been brought up to date where necessary, but are otherwise unchanged. I have also altered the content of the various appendices to discard information which is no longer required, and to include what I hope is currently useful information.

I would like to highlight one particular development and commend it whole-heartedly to you. It is that set out by Stephen Cobb in paragraphs 27.14 to 27.19, the so-called 'mini pupilage' scheme. As the text states, do not be put off by the name. There is no better introduction to the practice of family law than spending time sitting with an experienced Circuit or High Court judge. The Circuit Judges who have become Designated Family Judges (DFJs) and who are in charge of the various care centres up and down the country are, in my experience, remarkable people. They will, I anticipate, be welcoming and hospitable. A day spent in court sitting with one of them, or with one of the 19 specialist Family Division High Court judges, will, I am confident, be a day well spent and should do much to dispel any misapprehensions you may have about the courtroom as a working environment. All the information to enable you to spend such a day in a location convenient to yourself is contained in Chapter 27 and Appendices 2 to 4.

In this edition of the Handbook, you will find many more references to reported cases than appeared in the first edition. I have decided to refer to decided cases for several reasons. First of all, of course, they provide the full exposition of the propositions stated in the text. Secondly, as importantly, and as the note on page xvii makes clear, you will have ready access to the cases cited on the website of the British and Irish Legal Information Institute (BAILII), which is free. Chapter 36 is devoted to BAILII, and explains how the cases can be accessed. Do not be put off by their length. Judges are under an obligation to explain themselves fully, and their judgments are often long. You will, however, be able quite rapidly to distil the important messages, and as far as is possible, the Handbook will direct you to the relevant parts of each judgment.

You will also find that a bewildering amount of advice is now available from a wide variety of sources. The object of the Handbook is to distil the collective wisdom into a manageable format. This is not a book to be read from cover to cover at a sitting. It is there to dip into. I hope it will prove both helpful and reassuring to you, and I am grateful to the publishers for providing a detailed index. As with the previous edition, I would welcome feedback. Correspondence should be addressed to me at the Royal Courts of Justice, Strand, London, WC2A 2LL.

Any errors are, of course, my responsibility.

Nicholas Wall

October 2007

INTRODUCTION TO THE FIRST EDITION

This Handbook has three principal purposes. The first is to provide practical advice and guidance for expert witnesses instructed to prepare reports and give evidence in proceedings under the Children Act 1989 in England and Wales. The second is to encourage doctors and mental health professionals who have expertise in relation to children to undertake work in Children Act proceedings as expert witnesses. The third is to raise standards and harmonise good practice both amongst the judiciary making orders for expert evidence under the Children Act 1989, and amongst practitioners who seek such orders and then have to put them into effect.

Since the implementation of the Children Act 1989 in October 1991, there has undoubtedly been a growing reliance by the courts on expert evidence in the context of the physical and sexual abuse of children, as well as in cases of physical and emotional neglect and in relation to the assessment of children's relationships with their parents and the risks posed to children by any given placement. At the same time, the pool of experts willing and able to undertake the work is small and, in some parts of the country, for example on the Northern Circuit, demand substantially exceeds supply.

In the years since the implementation of the Children Act, there has also been a growth of case-law decided mostly by the Court of Appeal and the judges of the Family Division relating both to the jurisprudential basis upon which the courts approach expert evidence in proceedings relating to children, as well as practical issues such as time-tabling and report writing.

This handbook will seek to explain the way in which the courts hearing proceedings relating to children approach expert evidence. It aims to dispel misunderstandings and to help medical and mental health professionals to an awareness and understanding of the important legal developments which have been taking place. By these means, the book aims to encourage more suitably qualified experts to take on this very important work.

As a general rule, doctors do not read the law reports, and lawyers do not read medical journals. Thus, despite much excellent inter-disciplinary work and a number of good articles both in the legal and the medical press, there appears to be a continuing level of misunderstanding between the medical and legal professions about what is expected by the courts of expert witnesses in proceedings under the Children Act.

In particular, some experts seem unsure about what they can and cannot do both when preparing expert opinions for court and when appearing in court.

Equally, the legal profession continues from time to time to treat expert witnesses in a cavalier fashion, seeming to think that they can be called to court at will, and showing no understanding of their clinical responsibilities.

Expert witnesses are crucial to the proper operation of family proceedings. Courts are often dependent for their decisions on the quality of the medical evidence they receive and the integrity of those who give it. Through multi-disciplinary co-operation, judges and advocates increasingly understand that preparing a report and coming to court to give evidence are time-consuming and take doctors away from their clinical responsibilities. Efforts have been made by the judges to address these issues.

On the other side of the equation, many doctors still see the courtroom in family proceedings as a hostile environment, and some perceive the purpose of cross-examination as being to impugn their professional integrity by means of a personal attack on their credibility.

If this book can help to dispel myths and to help establish good practice, it will have achieved its objective. It encourages experts to be more proactive in their approach to report writing and not to feel that they are at the mercy of the judiciary and the legal profession.

Proceedings relating to children are in a special category of litigation. In the vast majority of cases, the welfare of the child is the court's paramount consideration. Expert witnesses must adopt the same approach. As the opening chapters of this book make clear, the expert instructed in Children Act proceedings writes an opinion for the court to assist the court in fulfilling its duty to the child. Thus, neither the partisan expert, nor the expert who has a particular hobby-horse to ride, is wanted in family proceedings.

Expert witnesses need to remember that most judges do not have anymore medical expertise than the average intelligent lay person. It is for this reason that they rely heavily on expert opinion, and are dependent upon the integrity of expert witnesses.

It is to be hoped that this book, which, for a trial period, will be supplied with the letter of instruction to all experts instructed to advise the courts in family proceedings on the Northern Circuit, will assist and reassure doctors about the importance of their role, and give them practical guidance about what they can and cannot properly do.

I am very conscious, from feedback which I have received that, in practice, many of the guidelines for good practice for lawyers which I have described in this book are not being followed on the ground. Aspirations are of no use if they are not implemented. This book will thus also be circulated to all the judiciary on circuit who hear family cases, and attempts will be made to ensure that it is read by lawyers practising in the field.

The text is addressed directly to experts in the second person plural in the hope that this will make it more immediately and apparently relevant. The chapter on fees has been contributed by Iain Hamilton, solicitor and Recorder.

I have, wherever possible, avoided direct references to decided cases in the text. A suggested reading list for further reference is given in Appendix 1.

A number of professional witnesses who read this book in manuscript suggested that it would be helpful to have a chapter giving some answers to specific questions which they had encountered in practice. In the event, space does not permit me to do this: in addition, I suspect that such a chapter would be like the 'Help' facility on most computer programs, which, frustratingly, never seems to address the particular problem with which you are wrestling. I have, therefore, attempted to deal with most of the issues which were suggested to me in the body of the text.

However, if this book does not answer practical questions or give experts the help they need, I hope that they will tell me so. Guidance such as I have offered in this book is not intended to be written in stone, and will benefit from being modified and updated. Comments and feedback from expert witnesses, the judiciary and practitioners will therefore be welcomed. Any correspondence should be addressed to me c/o the Circuit Administrator, Northern Circuit, 15 Quay Street, Manchester M60 9FD.

Nicholas Wall

March 2000

NOTE ON THE CASES REFERRED TO IN THE HANDBOOK AND ON REVISIONS TO THE PROTOCOL

THE CASES AND BAILII

I anticipate that very few of the medical readers of this Handbook will have access to the law reports or, even less likely, a subscription to one or more of the legal databases identified in Appendix 5. It is, therefore, very important that you should be able to have easy access to the cases which I identify in the Handbook. I also readily acknowledge that nothing is more frustrating than to spend valuable time searching the internet or a particular website for an item which turns out not to be there.

The publishers have therefore kindly agreed that although not all of the cases which I have cited currently have a neutral reference number, they will all appear on BAILII, and thus be accessible should you wish to read any of them in full or even in part. The use of BAILII is addressed in Chapter 36 of the Handbook.

This means that if you want to, you will be able to look up particular cases. I hope you will do so, as many of the extracts which I have cited simply do not do justice either to the difficult facts with which both you and the court have had to wrestle, or to the careful process of evaluation undertaken by the court.

The more you understand about the judicial thought process, the more valuable, I am sure, will be your contribution to the outcome of individual cases.

REVISIONS TO THE PROTOCOL

As envisaged by Ryder J in *W v Oldham MBC* (see, in particular, paragraphs **32.11** and **32.12** below and the footnote to paragraph **32.12**), Appendix C to the Protocol is being revised to incorporate the recommendations made in that case. The revision will take the form of a Practice Direction to be issued by the President as part of the forthcoming Public Order Outline. The draft Practice Direction is printed at Appendix 11. As stated in the introduction, you may safely assume that none of the principles which underlie either the Protocol or the proposed Public Law Outline is likely to change the basic guidance set out in this Handbook.

ACKNOWLEDGEMENTS

As ever, I owe debts of gratitude to a number of people who have contributed to the production of this edition of the Handbook.

Following Iain Hamilton's appointment to the Circuit Bench, the task of writing the chapter on fees has fallen to a busy London child specialist solicitor, Peggy Ray, and I am grateful to her for producing in Chapter 25 so coherent an analysis of what remains a changing and unsatisfactory situation for you.

I am also extremely grateful to Stephen Cobb QC for taking on the task of writing about the newly created Family Justice Council, which represents the culmination of a long struggle to establish a national body for the promotion and improvement of family law and practice. I therefore commend Chapter 27 and Appendix 2 to you. I particularly urge you to take up the opportunity to spend time sitting with an experienced Circuit or High Court Judge.

In relation to the Family Justice Council, I would also like to thank Dr Rosalyn Proops not only for reading the manuscript and bringing it to the attention of the President of the Royal College of Paediatrics and Child Health (RCPCH), but also for her enthusiastic promotion of a highly successful two-day court skills course which, I understand, is to be repeated in 2008.

I am grateful to Mr Justice Ryder for his invaluable contribution to the proposed revision of Appendix C of the Protocol (which deals with expert evidence and is reproduced as part of Chapter 26).

I am very grateful to the President of the Family Division, Sir Mark Potter, for his continuing support, and for writing a Foreword. I am equally very grateful to Dr Patricia Hamilton, the President of the RCPCH for taking the trouble to read the manuscript and for writing a Foreword.

I would also like to thank my clerk, Julie Baker, and Penelope Langdon, the President's Legal Secretary, for their help.

Finally, I owe a particular debt of gratitude to Professor Tim David, who has not only provided some of the material contained in this edition and read the manuscript, but who also made a wide variety of enormously helpful suggestions. It is no exaggeration to say that he is responsible for the current structure of the Handbook, and that much of the content owes a great deal to his rigorous analysis of, and comment upon, the original text.

I am no longer, of course, the Family Division Liaison Judge for the Northern Circuit. However, many of the ideas in the Handbook derive from my time in that role and much of the good practice which is now regarded as commonplace originates from practitioners in the North West. If I can no longer dedicate this edition to the practitioners of the Northern Circuit, it remains my hope that they will find it useful.

Any errors are, of course, my sole responsibility.

CONTENTS

Chapter 1

MEADOW v GENERAL MEDICAL COUNCIL (GMC)[1]

1.1   The whole of this first chapter of the Handbook is being devoted to *Meadow v GMC* for two very simple reasons. The first is because it is a very important decision for all expert witnesses; indeed, it sets the framework for many of the issues identified and discussed in this Handbook. The second, and equally important reason, is that you may be concerned about its implications for you as an expert witness. Self-evidently, you do not want to be reported to the GMC by a disaffected litigant or relative because of what you have written in a report to the court or stated in your oral evidence.

1.2   My assessment is that you do not need to be concerned. The decision of the Court of Appeal in *Meadow v GMC* does not change the law. Its principal messages for you are; (1) that experts in their reports and evidence should never stray outside the particular areas of their expertise; and (2) if you are invited to do so in your instructions to advise or in your evidence, you should either decline the invitation, or make it very clear to the judge that the area on which you are being invited to comment is not one to which your expertise extends. All three judges in the Court of Appeal repeat these two messages and all three refer with approval to the decision of Cresswell J in *The Ikarian Reefer* which forms the basis of Chapter 6 of this Handbook on your general duties to the court.

1.3   Thus the simple message of this Handbook remains the same and remains valid. I therefore repeat what I said in the introductions. Do your work conscientiously, and provided your report and your oral evidence are honest, fair and well reasoned, and provided always that you have worked within the area of your expertise, you have nothing to fear and much to gain from participating in family proceedings as an expert witness.

1.4   Clearly, however, *Meadow v GMC* is not as simple as this and it contains a number of lessons which you need to absorb. Thus, whilst I hope you will find this chapter helpful, there is no real alternative to reading the decision in full, despite the fact that it is very long (281 paragraphs).[2]

1.5   The context for *Meadow v GMC* was not, of course, litigation under the Children Act 1989. Professor Sir Roy Meadow (henceforth Professor Meadow) gave evidence for the prosecution at the trial of Mrs Sally Clark for the alleged murder of her two infant sons, both of whom had died suddenly and unexpectedly. His evidence was principally designed to refute the proposition that the two children's deaths were attributable to sudden infant death syndrome (SIDS), although, in the event, this was not in fact Mrs Clark's defence. Her case was that both deaths were from unknown natural causes.

1.6 In the course of his evidence, Professor Meadow made a number of references to statistics. This is the part of his evidence for which he was criticised. Mrs Clark was convicted, and appealed against her conviction to the Criminal Division of the Court of Appeal (CACD) (the first appeal). The CACD dismissed the first appeal. As Auld LJ put it in paragraph 101 of his judgment in *Meadow v GMC*:

> [101]   In 2000, Mrs Clark appealed unsuccessfully to the Court of Appeal against those convictions (*R v Clark* [2000] All ER (D) 1219, [2000] EWCA Crim 54). The court found the pathological and circumstantial evidence to be overwhelming proof of guilt, regardless of the various complaints made in the grounds of appeal, one of which went to Professor Meadow's use of the statistics. The court regarded that evidence as irrelevant to the issue whether the deaths of Mrs Clark's infants had been natural or unnatural, voiced no criticism of Professor Meadow as to his use of it, expressed some concern that the trial judge had not ruled it inadmissible or given a stronger warning to the jury about it than he did, but held that it did not, in the light of the other evidence, render the conviction unsafe.

1.7   Auld LJ then explained how Mrs Clark's second appeal arose:

> [102]   Subsequently, it was discovered that the pathologist, Dr Alan Williams, who had conducted the post mortem of Christopher and the initial post mortem of Harry, had not disclosed to the prosecution or at trial highly relevant results of certain biological tests on Harry. That led the Criminal Cases Review Commission to refer her case back to the Court of Appeal, which this time upheld her appeal. It did so, on the basis of that non-disclosure. It did not order a re-trial since the prosecution did not seek it, having regard to the fact that, if the non-disclosed material had been disclosed and considered at the time, it was likely that further tests, not possible years after the event, would have been undertaken. In the circumstances, the court did not need to, and did not, hear full argument or any evidence on the implications for the safety of her convictions of Professor Meadow's statistical evidence. Nevertheless, it expressed, albeit tentatively, some concern about the possible impact of that evidence on the jury, and stated that, if the point had been argued before the court, it would probably have provided 'a quite distinct basis upon which the appeal had to be allowed' (see [2003] EWCA Crim 1020 at [180], [2003] 2 FCR 447 at [180]).

1.8   Professor Meadow's evidence about statistics gave rise to a complaint to the GMC by Mrs Clark's father and to proceedings before the Fitness to Practice Panel (FPP) of the GMC. The outcome was a finding that Professor Meadow had been guilty of serious professional misconduct, and the penalty imposed by the GMC was the erasure of his name from the register.

1.9   Professor Meadow appealed to the High Court, where his appeal was allowed by Collins J.[3] The finding of serious professional misconduct was quashed and with it, of course, went the penalty of erasure. However, the judge decided, apparently of his own initiative, that expert witnesses enjoyed not merely immunity from civil suit[4] but also a wide, albeit not absolute immunity from disciplinary, regulatory or fitness to practice proceedings (collectively identified in the judgments as FTP proceedings) in relation to statements made or evidence given by them in or for the purpose of legal proceedings.

1.10   The GMC appealed to the Civil Division of the Court of Appeal against both Collins J's quashing of the finding of serious professional misconduct and his judgment that experts enjoyed immunity from FTP proceedings. It was this second finding which prompted the Attorney General to intervene. He argued that that the immunity identified by the judge did not exist. The Court of Appeal unanimously agreed with him and the GMC's appeal was allowed to that extent. Although the GMC had also appealed against the judge's decision that Professor Meadow had not been guilty of serious professional misconduct, it did not seek to reinstate the penalty of erasure. The Court of Appeal, by a majority (Auld and Thorpe LJJ, Sir Anthony Clarke, the Master of the Rolls[5] dissenting) held that, whilst guilty of professional misconduct, Professor Meadow had not been guilty of serious professional misconduct. No question of penalty therefore arose.

1.11   Several aspects of the case are striking and need to be noted. The first is that the FPP did not have before it either of the judgments of the Criminal Division of the Court of Appeal in Mrs Clark's case.[6] This was because of an agreement between leading counsel. Leading counsel for the GMC wanted the FPP to have the second judgment, which allowed the appeal, and quashed the conviction, but not the first, which had dismissed Mrs Clark's appeal. Leading counsel for Professor Meadow wanted the FPP to have before it the first judgment, in which Professor Meadow's evidence had been discussed, but not the second. The compromise they reached, which appears to have been accepted by the FPP, was that it should have neither. All three members of the Court of Appeal found this strange and Thorpe LJ in particular took the view that the FPP, as a result, had failed to understand the full context in which Professor Meadow had given evidence.[7]

1.12   The second striking aspect of the case is that there was no attack made at any point on Professor Meadow's primary evidence, namely his opinion that neither death was due to natural causes. Thus no criticism was made of the evidence given by Professor Meadow which was plainly within the area of his expertise.

1.13   Thirdly, as Auld LJ demonstrates in his judgment,[8] not only was there no objection taken by the defence to the admissibility of Professor Meadow's evidence relating to statistics on the ground that it was irrelevant or unfairly prejudicial; the defence in its cross-examination of Professor Meadow did not challenge either the underlying statistics relating to the chances of a child dying from SIDS (roughly 1 in 1,000) or the erroneous proposition that a second death from the same cause could be estimated statistically by squaring the initial figure. Counsel for Mrs Clark did challenge the figure of 1 in 8,543 as the chance of a child dying from natural causes as being too high, but did not cross-examine Professor Meadow on the erroneous proposition that the prospect of two children in the same family dying from natural causes could be calculated statistically by squaring the figure for one child – so that for a second child, the chances were 8,543 x 8,543, and thus 1 in 73 million.

1.14 The reason the CACD allowed the second appeal and quashed Mrs Clark's conviction was, of course, the fact that the Crown's pathologist had not disclosed material evidence to the defence, with the consequence that the jury's verdict was unsafe: see paragraph 102 of Auld LJ's judgment set out in paragraph **1.7** above. As a further consequence, full argument on Professor Meadow's evidence was not heard during the second appeal (as it had been during the first), although the court in the second appeal indicated that, had the point been argued, the appeal would 'in all probability' have been allowed on that ground also. A re-trial was not ordered for the obvious reason that had disclosure been made, as it should have been, other tests would have been conducted which were now impossible.

1.15 The upshot of *Meadow v GMC*, accordingly, is, in broad terms that the law remains as it was before the judgment of Collins J in the High Court was delivered. When acting as an expert witness, you, like everybody else, enjoy a general immunity from being sued in relation to what you say in court. However, you do not enjoy a wider immunity against action by your professional body if you have behaved unprofessionally. Furthermore, the judgments appear to confirm the advice consistently given by Family judges (and emphasised in the first edition of this Handbook) that, when giving expert evidence, you should never stray outside the particular area of your expertise.[9]

1.16 So what did Professor Meadow do wrong? Thorpe LJ sums up the majority opinion in paragraph 251 of the judgment when he says:

> [251]   In this appeal there can be no doubt that Professor Sir Roy Meadow fell short of the required standards. He advanced a probability theory that can only be applied in the calculation of the odds against the happening of two truly independent events. He was not expert in the calculation of probability. The calculation which he advanced in his original witness statement for the trial of Mrs Clark was drawn from a paediatric paper which he had published in the Archives of Disease in Childhood in 1999, without any citation of the source. In the days immediately preceding the trial he submitted a supplemental witness statement in which he advanced an even more extreme calculation drawn from the Confidential Enquiry into Stillbirths and Deaths in Infancy (CESDI) study by Professor Fleming and others. He knew from the text of the article that simple squaring was not a reliable basis for the calculation of the probability of recurrence given that two infant deaths within the same family are not independent events.

He, who had introduced the CESDI study to the case, allowed the bare table for the calculation of probability by squaring to go before the jury without the qualifications expressed in the accompanying text. When cross-examined, far from fairly admitting the need for qualification, he elaborated the figure produced by simple squaring with illustrations, one of which (backing an eighty to one Grand National winner in four consecutive years) he has subsequently acknowledged to be inappropriate and insensitive. Such breaches of the duties imposed upon an expert witness must amount to misconduct even if the witness had no intention to mislead and honestly believed in the validity of his opinion.

1.17 Both Auld and Thorpe LJJ were, however, unable to accept that in the context of the particular case Professor Meadow had been guilty of serious professional misconduct. It was common ground that Professor Meadow's erroneous evidence had been given in good faith, with no intent to mislead. Moreover, as Thorpe LJ points out in paragraph 252 of the judgment, at Mrs Clark's trial, the fundamental fallacy, namely that the recurrence of a second SIDS death in the same family could be calculated by simple squaring, was common ground between prosecution and defence. Moreover, Professor Berry, the author of the CESDI report was available to give evidence for the defence.

LESSONS TO BE LEARNED FROM THE CASE

1.18 The judgment given by Thorpe LJ in *Meadow v GMC*, in particular, repays study. In the opening section of his judgment, under the heading *Family Justice Background*,[10] he emphasises the importance of medical evidence in the area of child protection, and the substantial reliance which the court places on the professional integrity of the experts who advise it. He then goes on to point out that, in the field of family justice, demand for expert evidence exceeds supply. The system, he argues, is thus very sensitive to increasing or newly emerging disincentives. [11]

1.19 For all these reasons, therefore, the message of *Meadow v GMC* is clear. Although this was a case which had its roots in Mrs Clark's criminal trial and although different evidential rules apply in proceedings under the Children Act, expert evidence remains of critical importance. The law has not changed. Expert witnesses, like everyone else who gives evidence in court, cannot be sued for what they write in court reports or say in evidence. They do not, however, enjoy immunity from disciplinary proceedings before their respective professional bodies. And as explained later in this Handbook, the various duties which experts owe include the all-important consideration that they should not stray outside the particular area of their expertise.

1.20 What other lessons can we learn from *Meadow v GMC*? The first is that it is now a matter of urgency that the dearth of high quality medical evidence in child protection cases is properly addressed. Everyone engaged in the Family Justice System is aware of, and understands, your reluctance to become involved in giving evidence in public law cases under Part IV of the Children Act 1989. Quite apart from all the well known disincentives – the time-consuming nature of the work, the inconvenience of fitting it in with other clinical responsibilities, the disagreeable experience of your carefully articulated view being challenged in cross-examination, the need to travel long distances to give evidence, the risk that the case may not have been properly time-tabled in order to accommodate your evidence – comes the risk, highlighted in *Meadow v GMC* that you will be reported to your professional body by a disaffected party or one of his or her supporters.

1.21   It remains my firm view, however, that the chances of you being reported to your professional body are minimal if you follow the guidance given in *Meadow v GMC* and reiterated in this Handbook.

1.22   In addition, as this Handbook makes clear, efforts have undoubtedly been made by the legal profession and by the judiciary to address these problems. The best example is the Code of Guidance contained in Appendix C to the *Protocol for Judicial Case Management in Public Law Children Act cases*[12] *(the Protocol)* which sets out in considerable detail both the duties imposed on experts and the practicalities of ensuring that the maximum value is extracted from your evidence. As Thorpe LJ again points out in the same passage in his judgment in *Meadow v GMC*, valuable work was done in this area by the President's Interdisciplinary Committee and is now being done by the recently created Family Justice Council.[13]

1.23   Thorpe LJ also makes the point[14] which in my view is a very good one, that when, following the decision of the Criminal Division of the Court of Appeal in *R v Cannings*,[15] the government announced that there would be a review of past cases in which conviction or care orders had been made on the premises so severely criticised in *R v Cannings*, only two appeals were brought from care orders made in the Family Division, and both were dismissed.[16]

1.24   The reasons for this are not far to seek. Expert evidence in care proceedings in the Family Division is invariably subjected to rigorous scrutiny by the advocates and the judge. The process is quasi-inquisitorial / investigative, and a relaxation of the strict rules of evidence allows the judge to follow leads and ask questions not permitted in a criminal trial. Furthermore, the most difficult cases are heard either by the highly experienced High Court judges of the Family Division, or by Circuit judges and Recorders, most of whom have been empowered to sit in the High Court, and all of whom, in addition to their experience as advocates, have been through specific training relating to the hearing of care proceedings.

1.25   In addition, of course, the judge rarely reaches a conclusion in care proceedings on the expert evidence alone, or indeed on the evidence of a single expert. There is usually a body of expert evidence (sometimes conflicting) and the judge has to assess the whole picture, which includes findings of fact and assessments of credibility.[17]

1.26 Finally, the judge in Family Proceedings must give a judgment, explaining the conclusions the court has reached, and the role expert evidence has played in that conclusion. That judgment will often be made public and, if necessary, will be reviewed in public on appeal.

1.27 None of this, of course, is to say that mistakes are not made. Some of them are discussed in this Handbook.[18] Furthermore, the family justice system is over-stretched and under-resourced. The importance of the work, however, and the need for experts of high quality to give evidence in child protection cases cannot be over-emphasised.

1.28 One of the principal purposes of the first edition of this Handbook was to encourage expert witnesses like you to come forward and make themselves available to give evidence in family proceedings under the Children Act. That remains its principal purpose. The cause – child protection – is not only worthy: it is fundamental to the operation of the whole family justice system. Furthermore, it remains one in which you, as an expert witness, have a vital role. Once again, the importance of your role to the proper functioning of the system cannot be overstated.[19]

NOTES

[1]   The decision of the Court of Appeal was handed down on 26 October 2006 and is reported in a number of the law reports – see, for example, [2007] 1 FLR 1398, [2006] 3 FCR 447, [2007] 1 All ER 1. The neutral citation number is [2006] EWCA Civ 1390. The decision of Collins J at first instance was given on 17 February 2006 and is reported at [2006] 2 All ER 329 and [2006] 2 FCR 777. You will also find it on BAILII. The neutral citation number is [2006] EWHC 146 (Admin). To identify the relevant law reports and an explanation of the abbreviations used in related to them, see Appendix 5. To access both decisions on BAILII, see Chapter 36.

[2]   It has to be accepted that the length of any given judgment represents a powerful disincentive to read it in full. However, judges are obliged to give reasons for their conclusions, not least in order that the litigants in the case can understand why they have either succeeded or failed. They also have to set out the facts of the case – which are usually in dispute – as they have found them to be. The advantage of cases reported in the law reports is that they are edited, and invariably have a headnote, which sets out the salient facts, explains the issues and identifies the important parts of the judgment.

[3]   [2006] EWHC 146 (Admin). See also note 1 above.

[4]   Immunity from civil suit means that you cannot be sued for anything you say in court. Everybody enjoys immunity from civil suit for the simple reason that the courts wish to encourage people to give evidence in court without being fearful of the consequences if they have to say something strong about somebody else. However, immunity from suit is quite different from immunity from an accusation of professional misconduct if what you say in court offends against the rules of your professional body.

[5] For a discussion of judicial titles, see Appendix 5. The Master of the Rolls is the title given to the Head of the Civil Division of the Court of Appeal.

[6] The first is reported at [2000] All ER (D) 1219, [2000] EWCA Crim 54: the second is on BAILII at [2003] EWCA Crim 1020.

[7] [2006] EWCA Civ 1390 at paragraphs 268–70 where he said:

> [268]   With the advantage of hindsight it seems both extraordinary and disadvantageous to deny the panel both judgments of the Court Appeal (Criminal Division). Miss Davis naturally wanted the panel to have the advantage of the judgment in the first appeal, Mr Seabrook, who led for the GMC at the panel hearing, wanted the panel to have the judgment of the court in the second appeal. Apparently the resulting agreement between leading counsel was that neither judgment should go to the panel.
>
> [269]   The predictable outcome, in my judgment, was that the panel failed to understand the full context in which Professor Meadow gave evidence. Their reasons suggest that they never understood that Professor Meadow's evidence as to probabilities went to a non-issue at the conclusion of the evidence.
>
> [270]   It is also apparent that the panel regarded Professor Meadow as responsible for misleading the jury by the introduction of the squaring mechanism for the calculation of probability. It does not seem from their reasons that they understood that it was common ground between prosecution and defence that that was the correct mechanism. Had they had the judgment of the court on the first appeal they would have appreciated that a legitimate evaluation demonstrated: (a) the probability of a recurring SIDS death in one family was a side-show at the trial and (b) Professor Meadow's evidence, flawed though it was, fell far short of serious professional misconduct.

[8] See, in particular, paragraphs 129–58.

[9] See Chapter 6. The same message is repeated at various points in this Handbook and cannot be stated too often.

[10] Paragraphs 225–49.

[11] You may also take comfort from the following passage from Auld LJ's judgment:

> [204]   An expert, who is called to give, and gives evidence, of opinion or otherwise, on matters within his own professional knowledge and experience has an 'overriding duty' to the court to assist it objectively on matters within his expertise. He is also bound both by the ethical code and generally accepted standards of his profession. The former is expressly acknowledged in civil matters in r 35.3 of the Civil Procedure Rules, and has been usefully elaborated by Cresswell J in his much cited analysis in *National Justice Cia Naviera SA v Prudential Assurance Co Ltd, The Ikarian Reefer* [1993] 2 Lloyd's Rep 68 at 81–82. The same or similar principles have been applied for many years in criminal and family cases. There is clearly much overlap in the two categories of obligation, but, in the hurly-burly of the trial process, especially seen through the eyes of the expert witness they may not, in practice, always complement each other.
>
> [205]   Where the conduct of an expert alleged to amount to a professional offence under scrutiny by his professional disciplinary body arises out of evidence he has given to a court or other tribunal, it is, therefore, important that that body should fully understand, and assess his conduct in the forensic context in which it arose. Of great importance are the circumstances in which he came to give the evidence, the way in which he gave it, and the potential effect, if any, it had on the proceedings and their outcome. If the disciplinary body lacks information to enable it properly to assess the expert's conduct in that forensic context, or fails properly to take it into account, a court reviewing its determination, is likely to bring important insights of its own to the matter. Not least

among those should be an appreciation of the isolation of an expert witness, however seasoned in that role, in the alien confines of the witness box in an adversarial contest over which the judge and the lawyers hold sway.

[206]   In criminal or civil proceedings, it is for the parties' legal representatives and ultimately the judge, to identify before and at trial what evidence, lay or expert, is admissible and what is not. In the case of expert evidence, involving, as it often does, opinion evidence as to causation, it is critical that the legal representatives of the party proposing to rely on such evidence should ensure that the witness's written and oral evidence is confined to his expertise and is relevant and admissible to the important issues in the case on which he has been asked to assist. Equally, it is incumbent on the legal representatives on the other side not to encourage, in the form of cross-examination or otherwise, an expert to give opinion evidence which is irrelevant to those issues and/ or outside his expertise, and, therefore, inadmissible. And, throughout, it is for the judge, as the final arbiter of relevance and admissibility, to ensure that an expert is assisted or encouraged to keep within the limits of his expertise and does so relevantly to the issues in the case on which he is there to assist.

[207]   All of this is not to absolve the expert of responsibility from professional or forensic impropriety in the presentation and form of his evidence. As a medical expert, he should know his limits. In most instances, his knowledge and instincts in his particular field should alert him to confining his evidence to those limits and the true issues identified for the court by the legal representatives of the parties. However, the forensic process, in preparation and in action at trial, is not always as ordered and considered as it should be. The issues may not always be sufficiently carefully defined, or the evidence, lay and expert, adequately prepared and tailored in advance, to deal with them. The trial process itself can be unpredictable in direction. From time to time the questioners and the questioned can lose sight of the essential issues in exploring or 'trying out for size' areas of evidence that, on careful examination, have no bearing on the case. The line and pace of the questioning may leave little time for calm analysis by an expert witness called to deal with a variety of issues on one or more of which he is required to express an opinion that is, or he knows is, to be, challenged. The same may be said for those questioning him and, indeed for the judge who is trying to keep up with the evidence as it is given. In that, sometimes, fevered process, mistakes can be made, ill-considered assertions volunteered or analogies drawn by the most seasoned court performers, whatever their role.

12   Reported at [2003] 2 FLR 719 at 771–83, and reproduced in Chapter 26.

13   For the work of the Family Justice Council, see Chapter 27 and Appendix 2.

14   [2006] EWCA Civ 1390, at paragraph 230.

15   [2004] EWCA Crim 1.

16   See *Re U (Serious Injury: Standard of Proof); Re B* [2004] EWCA Civ 567, and *Re U (Re-opening of Appeal)* [2005] EWCA Civ 52.

17   Ibid.

18   See Chapter 32 which is devoted to *W Oldham MBC* [2005] EWCA Civ 1247; [2007] EWHC 136 (Fam).

19   You may also like to know that the President of the Family Division shortly intends to issue a further Practice Direction designed both to facilitate and to speed up the provision of information and documentation from the court to the GMC or other professional body in any case in which a complaint is made. This should enable the professional body in question swiftly to obtain access to relevant documents, including the court's judgment which, in turn, should include an analysis of your evidence.

Chapter 2

WHY AM I DOING THIS?

2.1   You find yourself instructed to write a report and appear in court in family proceedings under the Children Act 1989. This may be because you were the treating paediatrician in a suspected case of non-accidental injury, or because a second opinion is required on the treating doctor's diagnosis. It may be that you are a radiologist whose opinion is sought on the significance of X-rays or brain scans. It may be that you are a psychiatrist whose opinion is sought on whether or not a child has been sexually abused, or how contact is to be re-started between children and a parent whom they have not seen for a long time, and about whom they have been given information which is untrue. You may be a psychologist instructed to make an assessment of a parent's capacity to care for children in a case of chronic emotional or physical neglect. Depending upon your particular area of expertise, there may be a number of other reasons for your involvement in the case.

2.2   Writing a court report in proceedings under the Children Act 1989 and appearing in court in care proceedings may be a new experience for you. It may be unfamiliar territory. Finding the time to read the documents in the case, interviewing the parties and/or the child, writing your report and organising your diary to enable you to give evidence in court may all appear excessively time-consuming. Why are you doing it?

2.3   From the court's perspective, you are doing it because the court has asked you to, and has given permission for you to see the confidential papers in the case. A principal theme of this book is that, although your formal instructions come from the solicitors for one of more of the parties, you are being asked for your opinion because the court needs your expertise to help it reach a decision which is in the best interests of the child or children concerned.

2.4   Expert evidence is often of critical importance in a difficult child case. Sometimes it is determinative of a child's future. The court therefore places substantial reliance on the professional integrity of the experts who advise it. The point to bear in mind throughout is that you are involved in the case to assist the judge reach the right result for the child or children in the case. You are not there to support, or advance, the case of any of the adult parties. I make no apology for repeating this particular message at different points in this book.

2.5   Judges and lawyers increasingly recognise the demands which they make on expert witnesses. Good practice now requires that great care should be taken over the instruction of expert witness and the brief you are given.[1]

2.6   Efforts should also be made to ensure that you have sufficient time in which to prepare your opinion and that your court appearance is timetabled to fit in with your other professional commitments.

2.7   This book is concerned with what should be happening. It is one thing for judges to say what good practice should be – another to put it into effect. So you may still find that the lawyers who commissioned your report and fixed a date for you to give evidence fail to tell you that the case has been adjourned or that your evidence is no longer required, with the result that you turn up at court only to be sent away again – or get a message to that effect on your mobile telephone as you are on your way to court. You may still find that when you get to court you are kept hanging about, or asked to come back on another day. These are examples of bad practice which this book hopes to reduce and, in an ideal world, would be eliminated.

2.8   This book therefore aims to set out not only what is expected of expert witnesses in proceedings under the Children Act, but also what expert witnesses can reasonably expect from the court and from the lawyers involved in the case.

2.9   If your experience is that the good practice set out in this book is not being followed, it is important that you make your views known. If you have a bad experience, you should complain. Chapter 24 tells you how to do so. In addition, you should note that the Family Justice Council (FJC), described in detail by Stephen Cobb QC in Chapter 27 and Appendix 2, now provides you with an additional forum in which to voice your concerns. Whilst the FJC may not be able to investigate (and has no power to adjudicate upon) individual complaints, its Experts Committee is a forum for the discussion of issues relevant to expert evidence in the family courts – see paragraph **27.12**.

NOTE

[1]   See, in particular, Appendix C to the *Protocol for Judicial Case Management in Public Law Children Act Cases* set out in Chapter 26.

Chapter 3

THE NATURE OF FAMILY PROCEEDINGS RELATING TO CHILDREN

3.1 Family Proceedings relating to children under the Children Act 1989 are divided into two categories. The first, which are governed by Part II of the Act, are commonly called 'private law' proceedings. These mostly concern disputes between separated parents over their children – most frequently where and with whom they should live, and how much contact the non-resident parent should have with them. The crucial aspect of private law proceedings is that, usually, neither the local authority nor any other public authority is involved in the case, although an officer of the Children and Family Court Advisory and Support Service (CAFCASS) [1] is frequently invited by the court to report to it on the dispute between the parents.

3.2 Public law proceedings, which are governed by Part IV of the Act, are nearly always concerned with whether or not a child should be taken temporarily or permanently into the care of a particular local authority. That local authority is nearly always the applicant in the proceedings. In very broad terms, the position is that before the court can make a care order under section 31 of the Children Act, two principal conditions must be fulfilled. Firstly, the local authority must satisfy the court that at the time it took the proceedings, the child concerned was suffering or was likely to suffer 'significant harm' attributable to the care (or lack of care) provided by his parents. These are the so called 'threshold criteria' contained in section 31 of the Act. If they are not satisfied, that is the end of the proceedings. If they are satisfied, the court can then only go on to make a care order if it takes the view that such an order is better for the child than making no order, and that a care order is in the child's best interests.

3.3 Parliament has not provided a definition of 'significant harm' and the courts have been free to give the words their natural meaning when applied to the facts of any particular case.

3.4 Like private law proceedings, care proceedings can be heard in any level of court. You are, however, much less likely to be instructed to advise in care proceedings pending before magistrates in the Family Proceedings Court (FPC) because although all care proceedings have to start in the FPC, complex cases involving expert evidence and other medical issues are usually transferred up to the County Court or the High Court, where they are heard by a specialist judge or recorder.

3.5   The Family Division of the High Court retains what is known as its 'inherent jurisdiction' over children. This includes 'wardship'. The legal theory behind both is that the High Court exercises what used to be called a 'parens patriae' jurisdiction over those who were incapable of caring for themselves. Thus the High Court retains a power in certain circumstances to override the decisions normally taken by a child's parents. The most common cases are those in which doctors take the view that the child should either undergo a particular form of treatment with which the child's parents do not agree – or vice versa. There are many of these cases in the law reports, but they are unlikely to concern you unless you are the treating physician whose judgment is challenged by a child's parents, or you are called in to advise on the appropriateness of the treatment in question.[2]

3.6   You are much more likely to be instructed to advise in public law proceedings than in private law proceedings. This is for a number of reasons, not least amongst them being the fact that public funding is more readily available in public law proceedings, and because the child is invariably separately represented by a solicitor and a guardian. It is also because the question of whether or not the child has suffered or is likely to suffer significant harm frequently involves medical and mental health issues.

3.7   This Handbook is not concerned with criminal proceedings, although it may well be that you will find yourself involved in them, either giving evidence for the prosecution or for the defence.[3] Sometimes, both criminal and family proceedings arise out of the same set of facts – for example where care proceedings are taken in relation to a child who has been the subject of a criminal assault, or where parents are prosecuted over the death of a child and care proceedings are taken in relation to a sibling, who is thought to be at risk of significant harm. The interface between criminal and family proceedings is addressed in Chapter 16.

3.8   However, whatever the nature of the proceedings, the essential rules relating to expert evidence, and the principles which should guide you in providing evidence for the court, are exactly the same. The chapters which follow will be devoted to explaining them.

NOTES

[1]   For an explanation of the role of CAFCASS in family proceedings, see Appendix 10.

[2]   Perhaps the most well-known recent example is the series of decisions involving the dispute between the parents of Charlotte Wyatt and the hospital treating her, starting with *Portsmouth NHS Trust v Wyatt* [2004] EWHC 2247 (Fam), [2005] 1 FLR 21, in which the

judge upheld the medical opinion that it was not in the child's interest to be ventilated in certain circumstances.

3   Apart from important differences in the rules of evidence, one of the principal differences between criminal and family proceedings is that a defendant in criminal proceedings is entitled to claim legal professional privilege over any report you have written for the criminal proceedings: see *S County Council v B* [2000] 2 FLR 161. However, your approach to your task should not differ and most of the differences are for lawyers, not for you.

Chapter 4

THREE CARDINAL PRINCIPLES GOVERNING FAMILY PROCEEDINGS

4.1 Three cardinal principles underlie the approach of the court to expert evidence in family proceedings and it is very important that you should understand all three, as they govern the approach which the court will expect you to adopt in writing your report and in giving evidence. The three principles are:

(1) **The proceedings are non-adversarial**.
This means that the court is not concerned with whether one side or the other will succeed in achieving the result which that side wants. The court is concerned with the welfare of the children who are the subject of the proceedings. Their welfare is the court's paramount consideration and the views and aspirations of the other parties to the proceedings are relevant only insofar as they reflect on the welfare of the children involved.

(2) **The proceedings are confidential**.
Statements and other papers generated by the court process in family proceedings are confidential to the court and, with very few exceptions, it is a contempt of court to disclose them to a person who is not a party to the proceedings without the court's permission.[1] It follows that an expert can be instructed and shown the court papers only with the permission of the judge who, in turn, decides both what issues require expert evidence and the brief the expert should be given.
Furthermore, the Family Proceedings Rules 1991 provide, by rule 4.18(1) that 'no person may, without the leave of the court, cause the child to be medically or psychiatrically examined, or otherwise assessed, for the purpose of the preparation of expert evidence for use in the proceedings'.[2]

(3) **Litigation privilege does not apply**.
This means that a party who has commissioned a report from an expert witness cannot refuse to disclose the report to the judge and to the other parties to the proceedings. Whatever the report contains and whether or not it supports the case being put forward by the party who commissioned it, it must be disclosed. This is a very important consideration and in this respect, proceedings relating to children differ from other civil litigation. In most civil cases, including family proceedings relating to financial provision, the parties have the choice not to rely on the report of an expert witness

whom they have commissioned to write a report and in these circumstances they need not produce the report. This is not the case in proceedings relating to children. Whatever you write in your report will be disclosed to the court.

WHAT THESE PRINCIPLES MEAN FOR THE EXPERT WITNESS

4.2   The three principles I have identified are all fundamental to the way in which you should approach your task if you are instructed in family proceedings.

Non-adversarial

4.3   The phrase 'non-adversarial' should not be misunderstood. Of course there will be issues of fact in family proceedings which the court will have to decide on the balance of probabilities in the normal way.[3] Most expert evidence goes to factual issues. Obvious examples are: has this child been sexually abused? Was this a non-accidental injury? If it was, what was the likely timing and mechanism of the injury?

4.4   Medical evidence which goes to issues such as these will be tested in the normal way by cross-examination and the judge will have to decide, on the balance of probabilities, what happened. The importance of the non-adversarial principle for you is that you are not there to support one side or the other. You are there to give your objective professional opinion to the judge on the points which are within the area of your expertise in order to assist the judge to reach a conclusion which is in the best interests of the child or children concerned.

4.5   Family proceedings thus have a quasi investigative / administrative quality in which the court seeks the outcome which will best promote, or be least detrimental to, the welfare of the child. For this reason, the strict rules of evidence are relaxed and hearsay evidence is admissible.[4]

4.6   For these reasons, you owe your duty to the court and to the children involved in the case, not to the party who commissioned the report from you. You report to the judge and when you are called to give evidence, you give your evidence to the judge.

Confidentiality

The confidentiality of the proceedings

4.7   This phrase also should not be misunderstood. What it means is that the information contained in the papers filed with the court for the purposes of the proceedings is confidential to the court. Thus, with very few exceptions,[5] the court papers can be disclosed to people who are not parties to the proceedings only with the court's permission and publication outside the proceedings of information relating to the proceedings is in most cases a contempt of court unless permission for it has first been given by the court.

4.8   The fact that the court papers are confidential does not, however, prevent you from discussing the case with other experts or professionals engaged in the case. This topic is covered in more detail in Chapters 12 and 13.

4.9   Confidentiality, as discussed in this chapter, is not to be confused with the confidential relationship between patient and doctor. It does *not* mean that, in the course of your enquiries, parties to the proceedings or any witnesses whom you interview can tell you anything 'in confidence' which cannot then be revealed to the court. Rather to the contrary, there is no such thing as an 'off the record' discussion for an expert instructed in proceedings relating to children. Any piece of information which you obtain during the course of your enquiries which is relevant to your report must be disclosed in it.

4.10   It has to be recognised in the context of proceedings relating to children that, for example, the inability of a parent to provide information 'in confidence' to an expert may cause difficulties both for the parent and the expert. Parents, when you interview them, may wish to behave as they would in a medical consultation and give you confidential information which they might not provide in other circumstances. They may also be inhibited in telling you the truth for fear of a criminal prosecution if incriminating admissions are made.

4.11   For your purposes, however, the rule is clear. You are making enquiries within the proceedings for the purpose of making a report to the court. If, in these circumstances, you obtain information which is relevant to the welfare of the children with whom the court is concerned, it must be shared with the other parties to the proceedings and given to the court. It will then be for the court to decide if it should be passed on to any third party such as the police.[6]

Disclosure

4.12   Your report will be disclosed to the judge, to the other parties to the proceedings and to any other experts instructed in the case, irrespective of whether or not it supports the case of the party who commissioned it.

4.13   Disclosure has the following particular implications for you.

(1) The court will expect your report to be objective and wholly free from bias. You must avoid any attempt to write a report which is inappropriately slanted towards the commissioning party. Such an approach will be deprecated by the court and will devalue your evidence.

(2) Because the report will be read not only by the judge but by the other parties and any other experts instructed in the case, it is very important that it should address clearly the issues you have been instructed to address; that it should

be thorough, well reasoned and researched; and that the methodology you have used should be properly explained.

(3) The key concepts for you are openness and sound preparation. Remember that your work is likely to be subjected to a fair, but rigorous, analysis and challenge. It is, therefore, very important that your methodology is transparent. Remember also that everything you do or say is likely to be recorded in one form or another. Any letters you write relating to the case are liable to be disclosed. When you talk to the solicitor instructing you, he or she will make a note of the conversation (called 'an attendance note'), which may well be produced during the course of the case. So, if you have an important conversation with a solicitor, ask him or her to send you a copy of the attendance note he or she will have made. If you disagree with the content of the attendance note, tell the solicitor so in writing. Make sure that your own notes of meetings or interviews with the parties or the child are contemporaneous, full and accurate. A parent's barrister may well be instructed to challenge your version of a conversation. Be prepared for that to happen.

(4) The fact that your work will be subject of close examination should not deter you. What you are doing is very important and may well have substantial implications for the lives of the children and adults in the case. A principal message of this book is that if your work is conscientiously undertaken, your methodology sound and your conclusions well reasoned, it is highly unlikely that there will be any adverse consequences for you. Indeed, you may find the work you are doing is not only stimulating and very important; you may even find parts of it enjoyable!

SUMMARY

4.14   If you are instructed to write a report in family proceedings, your duty is to the court and to the child, not to the party who commissions the report. You cannot receive information 'in confidence' from anybody. All relevant information must be shared with the other parties and the court. Your report will be disclosed whatever it says. Your duty is to be objective and wholly free from bias in favour of one party or the other. Your watchwords should be openness and sound preparation. You must be prepared for everything you do and say to be the subject of challenge. If you do your work conscientiously, if your methodology is transparent and if your reports are objectively sound, it is highly unlikely that you will be the subject of any sustainable criticism.

NOTES

[1]   The exceptions arise because in *Re B (a child) (Disclosure)* [2004] EWHC 411 (Fam); [2004] 2 FLR 142 Munby J gave a wide meaning to the word 'publication' and decided (in particular)

that it was a contempt of court for confidential information relating to family proceedings to be disclosed by a party to his or her MP. This led the government to amend section 97(2) of the Children Act 1989 (which deals with privacy for children involved in family proceedings). Although the Family Proceedings Rules now allow a greater degree of disclosure for specified purposes, the changes do not affect expert witnesses and you should proceed on the basis that the documents disclosed to you are wholly confidential. The circumstances in which parties and witnesses (including experts) can be identified in discussed in Chapter 35.

2   Although the 1991 rules are in the process of being replaced by what will be called 'the Family Procedure Rules', it is unlikely that the rules relating to the medical or psychiatric examination of children will be changed.

3   For a discussion of the burden and standard of proof in cases under the Children Act 1989 see paragraph **5.9** et seq.

4   Hearsay evidence, as its name suggests, is material derived not from the direct actions, observations or experience of the witness but from what that witness has heard or read or derived from another source. Children rarely give oral evidence in family proceedings. Thus, the commonest example of hearsay evidence in such proceedings is the report by an adult of what the child has said – for example about an injury or abuse. As a general rule, the criminal law does not admit hearsay evidence, so that where an alleged abuser of a child is prosecuted, the child is required to give oral evidence and be cross-examined.

5   See note 1.

6   Section 98 of the Children Act 1989 does give parents some protection against self-incrimination. It provides that, in proceedings under the Act, no one can be excused from giving evidence, or answering any question whilst giving evidence, on the ground that the answer may incriminate them or their spouse, but that any such statement or admission made in the proceedings is not admissible in evidence in any other criminal proceedings against them or their spouse apart from perjury. However, where a father made an admission in care proceedings that he had caused injuries to a child leading to that child's death, the Court of Appeal ordered disclosure to the police of a transcript of his evidence on the basis that the public interest in the administration of justice overrode the public interest in confidentiality and frankness in proceedings relating to children: see *Re C (A Minor) (Care Proceedings Disclosure)* [1997] Fam 76. However, if you come across material in the course of your enquiries which, in your professional judgment, you think should be disclosed to the police or to any child protection agency, the fact that the proceedings are confidential does not prevent you doing so. If this happens, however, you should take immediate steps to inform the solicitor instructing you what you have done and why.

Chapter 5

THE RESPECTIVE ROLES OF EXPERT AND JUDGE: WHY THE PROFESSIONAL INTEGRITY OF EXPERTS IS SO IMPORTANT

5.1 It will help you, when writing a report and giving evidence in family proceedings, if you bear in mind throughout, the respective functions of expert and judge.

5.2 You form an assessment and express your opinion within the particular area of your expertise. Judges decide particular issues in individual cases on all the evidence available to the court.

5.3 Your function is to advise the judge. You do not decide the case or any issue in the case.[1] This is of particular relevance when the credibility of an adult witness is in question. Whether or not an adult witness is telling the truth is a matter for the judge, not for you.[2]

5.4 The corollary to this is that it is not for the judge to become involved in medical controversy except in the extremely rare case where such a controversy is itself an issue in the case and a judicial assessment of it becomes necessary for the proper resolution of the proceedings.[3]

5.5 The reason for judges avoiding medical controversy is obvious. Whilst most family judges have knowledge and experience from practice and previous cases, they rarely have more medical knowledge than the intelligent lay person. Judges, almost by definition, are not experts in the field about which you are giving evidence.

5.6 Judges bring to the inquiry forensic and analytical skills and have the unique advantage over the parties and the witnesses in the case that they alone are in a position to weigh all its multifarious facets. In *Re U (Serious Injury: Standard of Proof); Re B*,[4] the Court of Appeal stressed the importance of the court deciding cases on all the information available to it, not just on the expert evidence. This process, of course, involves (but is by no means limited to) an evaluation of your opinion in the context of the court's duty to make findings of fact and assessments of the credibility of witnesses.

5.7 It follows that the dependence of the court on the skill, knowledge and, above all, the professional and intellectual integrity of the expert witness cannot be over-emphasised. Judges have a difficult enough task as it is in sensitive child cases. To have, in addition, to resolve a subtle and complex medical disagreement or to make assessments of the reliability of expert witnesses not only adds immeasurably to the judges' task, but given their fallibility and lack of medical training, may help to lead them to false conclusions.

5.8   It is partly for this reason that the current practice of the courts in children cases is to require disclosure of all medical reports and to invite the experts to confer pre-trial.[5] It has been said that in deciding children's cases, judges need all the help they can get.[6]

THE STANDARD OF PROOF

5.9   Although it is for judges to decide what happened in cases where the facts are in dispute, your opinion will often be a crucial element in helping the judge form a view. The obvious example is an injury to a child which a parent claims has an innocent cause. It is for the judge to decide:

(1) how and when the injury occurred; and
(2) who was responsible for it.

Your role is nearly always limited to helping the judge on (1).

5.10   Judges decide disputed issues of fact in proceedings under the Children Act on the civil standard of proof known as 'the balance of probability'. This is a lower standard than that used in criminal proceedings to decide guilt, which is 'beyond reasonable doubt'.

5.11   The balance of probability test means simply that a court can be satisfied that an event occurred if it considers that, on the evidence before the court, the occurrence of the event was more likely than not.

5.12   However, in *Re H (Minors) (Sexual Abuse: Standard of Proof)*,[7] a decision of the House of Lords, the majority opinion was that certainty was seldom attainable and probability was an unsatisfactorily vague criterion because there were degrees of probability. Lord Nicholls of Birkenhead, giving the majority opinion, therefore added a rider to the 'balance of probability test' to the effect that the more serious or improbable the allegation of abuse, the more convincing was the evidence required to prove the allegation.[8]

5.13   This decision has relevance for you only insofar as you may be asked, for example, to express an opinion on the degree of likelihood or probability of an injury having been caused in a particular way or – to take another example – whether a child has been sexually abused. You should not be troubled by this. The process of differential diagnosis requires the systematic evaluation of the clinical evidence and diagnoses of different conditions are reached with differing degrees of confidence.

5.14   In the context of a finding of fact to be made by a judge, the safest way of expressing your opinion about a particular injury or condition is to say that it is 'consistent' or 'inconsistent' with a given set of facts. Plainly, however, degrees of likelihood are also involved in this analysis. Some clinical signs are pathognomonic of abuse. In such a case, you are entitled to say that the condition is consistent only with abuse.[9]

5.15   The *Re H* test is, of course, for lawyers, not for doctors If you find its analysis helpful in forming a diagnosis, you should feel free to adopt it. Essentially, however, what the judge is looking for is your clinical assessment and an opinion or diagnosis based on your clinical expertise.

SUMMARY

5.16   Judges decide cases while experts advise them on points specifically within the area of the expert's expertise. Judges rely heavily on the integrity of experts and encourage experts to agree whenever that is possible. Judges are not equipped to engage in medical controversy. Judges decide disputed factual issues on the balance of probability. Where the case concerns an injury to a child, the function of the expert is to advise the judge whether the injuries are consistent with particular facts or a particular explanation.

NOTES

[1]   This remains the case even if the question on which you are asked to advise turns out to be the very question which the judge has to decide.

[2]   See Chapter 7, in which this point is discussed more fully.

[3]   Because, for example, there have been disagreements between doctors about both causation and the force required for brain injuries in infants, judges have been required to become involved in the difficult question of the causation of such injuries in young children. This is, however, very much the exception. See, in this respect, Chapter 34.

[4]   [2004] EWCA Civ 567. See, in particular, the judgment of the court at paragraphs 22–27.

[5]   See further Chapters 12 and 13 and Appendix C to the Protocol set out in Chapter 26.

[6]   *Re M and R (Child Abuse: Evidence)* [1996] 2 FLR 195 at 205H to 206A per Butler-Sloss LJ.

[7]   [1996] AC 563.

[8]   The relevant passage in the speech of Lord Nicholls reads as follows:

   'The balance of probability standard means that a court is satisfied an event occurred if the court considers that, on the evidence, the occurrence of the event was more likely than not. When assessing the probabilities the court will have in mind as a factor, to whatever extent is appropriate in the particular case, that the more serious the allegation the less likely it is that the event occurred and, hence, the stronger should be the evidence before the court concludes that the allegation is established on the balance of probability. Fraud is usually less likely than negligence. Deliberate physical injury is usually less likely than accidental physical injury. A stepfather is usually less likely to have repeatedly raped and had non-consensual oral sex with his under age stepdaughter than on some occasion to have lost his temper and slapped her. Built into the preponderance of probability standard is a generous degree of flexibility in respect of the seriousness of the allegation.'

In the aftermath of *Re H*, there was a suggestion that the difference between the civil and the criminal standard of proof in cases involving the deaths of, or serious injuries to children was 'largely illusory'. However, in *Re T (Abuse: Standard of Proof)* [2004] EWCA Civ 558, the Court of Appeal firmly rejected this suggestion and re-affirmed that in all family cases relating to children, the standard of proof remained the balance of probabilities as stated by Lord Nicholls in *Re H*.

[9]   See also *Re B (Non-accidental injury)* 2002 EWCA Civ 752 noted in paragraph **34.5**.

Chapter 6

THE GENERAL DUTIES OF EXPERTS

6.1 The general duties which you owe when writing opinions for use in court and when giving evidence are very clear and apply in every type of proceedings. They were well expressed by Mr Justice Cresswell sitting in the Commercial Court in 1993 in a case known as *The Ikarian Reefer*.[1]

6.2 Mr Justice Cresswell said that the duties and responsibilities of expert witnesses included the following:

(1) Expert evidence presented to the court should be and seen to be the independent product of the expert uninfluenced as to form or content by the exigencies of litigation.
(2) An expert witness should provide independent assistance to the court by way of objective unbiased opinion in relation to matters within his expertise. An expert witness in the High Court should never assume the role of advocate.
(3) An expert witness should state the facts or assumptions on which his opinion is based. He should not omit to consider material facts which detract from his concluded opinion.
(4) An expert witness should make it clear when a particular question or issue falls outside his expertise.
(5) If an expert's opinion is not properly researched because he considers that insufficient data is available then this must be stated with an indication that the opinion is no more than a provisional one.

If after exchange of reports, an expert witness changes his view on a material matter, such change of view should be communicated to the other side without delay and when appropriate to the court.

Where expert evidence refers to photographs, plans, calculations, survey reports or other similar documents these must be provided to the opposite party at the same time as the exchange of reports.

PARTICULAR DUTIES IN FAMILY PROCEEDINGS

6.3 In relation specifically to family proceedings, the most important statement of principle remains that found in *Re R*,[2] a decision of Mr Justice Cazalet in

1991, in which, referring specifically to family cases, he said:

(1) Expert witnesses are in a privileged position: indeed, only experts are permitted to give an *opinion* in evidence. Outside the legal field the court itself has no expertise and for that reason frequently has to rely on the evidence of experts.

(2) Such experts must express only opinions which they genuinely hold and which are not biased in favour of one particular party. Opinions can, of course, differ and indeed quite frequently experts who have expressed their objective and honest opinion will differ, but such differences are usually within a legitimate area of disagreement.

(3) Experts should not mislead by omission. They should consider all the material facts in reaching their conclusions and must not omit to consider the material facts which could detract from their concluded opinion.

(4) If experts look for and report on factors which tend to support a particular proposition or case, their report should still:
 (a) provide a straightforward, not a misleading opinion;
 (b) be objective and not omit factors which do not support their opinion; and
 (c) be properly researched.

(5) If the expert's opinion is not properly researched because he or she considers that insufficient data is available, then the expert must say so and indicate that the opinion is no more than a provisional one.

(6) In certain circumstances, experts may find that they have to give opinions adverse to the party which instructed them. Alternatively if, contrary to the appropriate practice, an expert does provide a report which is other than wholly objective – that is one which seeks to 'promote' a particular case – the report must make this clear. However, such an approach should be avoided because it would (a) be an abuse of the position of the expert's proper function and privilege and (b) render the report an argument, not an opinion.

6.4   The principles set out by Mr Justice Cresswell and Mr Justice Cazalet are now uniformly accepted in all civil proceedings. You will find them in various forms in various different places. Your own professional body may have formulated its own version. The fact that they are generally accepted stresses their importance.[3]

THE DANGERS ARISING FROM A MISLEADING OR TENDENTIOUS OPINION: THE DUTY NOT TO MISLEAD

6.5   You should always bear in mind that a misleading opinion may inhibit a proper assessment of a particular case by the non-medical professional advisers and may also lead parties and, in particular, parents to false views and hopes.

6.6 Furthermore, such misleading expert opinions are likely to increase costs by requiring competing evidence to be called at the hearing on issues which should in fact be non-contentious.

6.7 In cases relating to children, your duty to be objective and not to mislead is especially vital because the child's welfare, which is paramount, is at stake. An absence of objectivity on your part may lead a judge to reach the wrong conclusion. It may, for example, result in a child being wrongly placed or otherwise unnecessarily at risk.[4]

SUMMARY

6.8 What the court expects from you is an objective, independent, well-researched, thorough opinion, which takes account of all relevant information and which represents your genuine professional view on the issues submitted to you.

NOTES

1   More fully, *National Justice Compania Naviera SA v Prudential Assurance Co Ltd* [1993] 2 Lloyd's Rep 68. They are also set out in Annex C to the Public Law Protocol – see Chapter 26.   In other civil proceedings (that is non-criminal proceedings, but excluding family cases), the court's powers to permit and control expert evidence are now codified in Part 35 of the Civil Procedure Rules 1998. In due course, the Family Procedure Rules will contain their own provisions governing the use of expert evidence in family proceedings. In the meantime, the essential guidance for experts in proceedings relating to children is as set out in the text of the Handbook. Reference can also be made to the Family Proceedings Rules 1991 (as amended) and to Appendix C to the *Public Law Protocol*.

2   See *Re R (A Minor) (Experts' Evidence)* [1991] 1 FLR 291.

3   As pointed out in Chapter 1, all three judges in *Meadow v GMC* cited with approval the judgment of Cresswell J in the *Ikarian Reefer*.

4   The case of *Re R* itself is a good example of the difficulties with which a judge can be faced when experts write reports designed to assist the party by whom they are instructed. In that case, which is only fully reported in the Family Court Reporter for 1991 at page 193, the judge found as a fact that one of the parents of a baby had severely shaken her. Apart from extensive brain damage, the child had five fractured ribs and numerous fractures to all four limbs. Four experts were called on the parents' behalf, one of whom was a psychiatrist. The three other doctors each suggested that the child's injuries could have an innocent explanation. A consultant neuroradiologist suggested that 'excessively poor mineralization of her skeleton at birth' could have led to an unspecified metabolic bone disorder. This was a suggestion which ignored the brain injuries and the neuroradiologist withdrew it in his oral evidence. A consultant paediatrician reported that it was possible that coughing had caused the rib fractures – a suggestion which he also withdrew in oral evidence, accepting that in this case the sub-dural haematoma suffered by the child was consistent only with trauma. A doctor involved in clinical research in relation to bone disease also advised that the child had brittle bones. The third doctor was also the subject of severe criticism in two later cases: *Re AB (Child Abuse: Expert Witnesses)* [1995] 1 FLR 181 and *Re X (Non-Accidental*

Injury: Expert Evidence) [2001] 2 FLR 90, [2001] EWHC Fam 1 and has since been struck off. The dangers of an expert with a particular standpoint ignoring important medical evidence and either seeking to fit the facts of the case into a particular medical theory or writing an opinion designed to exculpate the person who has commissioned the report cannot be overstated.

Chapter 7

WHAT YOU CAN ADVISE THE JUDGE ABOUT

7.1   As stated in Chapter 6, your function is to give your advice to the court on any issue properly within the area of your expertise. You do not decide the case: that is the function of the judge.

7.2   By virtue of section 3(1) of the Civil Evidence Act 1972, your opinion on any relevant matter on which you are qualified to give expert evidence is admissible in evidence.[1]

7.3   Accordingly, whilst it is for the judge to decide, for example, whether a child has been sexually abused, or is to be believed when recounting allegations of sexual abuse, you are entitled, if you have the relevant expertise, to tell the judge that in your opinion the child has been sexually abused or that the child is credible when he or she relates allegations of abuse.[2]

7.4   You should, however, be very cautious when advising a judge that in your opinion a particular event occurred. You should do this only if you feel you have all the relevant information and that the expression of such an opinion is both truly within the area of your expertise and a necessary part of your decision-making process. The judge will have to decide the question on all the evidence in the case, including the oral evidence given in the witness box. You will not have access to all that information and the expression of a categorical opinion which may be invalidated by material not within your knowledge will – at the very least – substantially devalue your evidence. Equally, you should not normally express an opinion about whether or not a witness is telling the truth. Adult credibility is a matter for the judge, not the expert witness. However, if your assessment of an adult either depends upon or has been influenced by your assessment of that person's credibility, you should say so and explain why you have reached the conclusion you have.[3]

7.5   If you are a paediatrician, it is most likely that you will be giving your evidence in the context of the judge's necessary findings of fact – for example – were the child's injuries non-accidental? However, the court sometimes needs expert assistance when deciding outcome. Thus – to take another example – a psychiatrist can properly give evidence of the likely outcome of a proposal that children be returned permanently to their parents' care.

SUMMARY

7.6   You are free to express an opinion about any issue in the case, including those which it is the province of the judge to decide, provided your expression of opinion relates to a matter on which you are qualified to give expert evidence. You should, however, be cautious about expressing firm opinions on events which may or may not have occurred and about which you may not have all the relevant information. You should also be very wary of expressing any opinion on whether or not a particular adult witness is telling the truth. This is something for the judge, not you, to decide.

NOTES

¹   This reads: 'Subject to any rules of court made in pursuance of this Act, where a person is called as a witness in any civil proceedings, his opinion on any relevant matter on which he is qualified to give evidence shall be admissible in evidence'. For an interesting recent example of the judicial perception of the division between judicial and clinical responsibilities, see the case of *Re M-M (a child)* [2007] EWCA Civ 589 (16 May 2007) discussed fully at paragraph **33.2**, note 1.

²   Note, however, that questions of adult credibility are for the judge and not for you – see, in particular, Chapter 30 on the courts' attitude to psychometric testing.

³   Thus, for example, if a judge has conducted a fact-finding hearing and has decided that a particular event occurred, or that a parent has not been telling the truth about an issue on which you are then asked to advise, it is not open to you to write a report on the basis that the particular event did not occur, or that the parent in question had been telling the truth. The facts of the case must be taken as found by the judge, unless you are in possession of compelling evidence which was not available to the judge and which points conclusively in the opposite direction.

Chapter 8

PRELIMINARY ENQUIRIES OF THE EXPERT

8.1 The first enquiry about the feasibility of you giving an opinion in a case will usually come from a solicitor acting for one of the parties including, of course, the solicitor who is acting for the child. It will often take the form of a telephone call enquiring about your availability to do the work within a given time-frame and giving only a broad outline of what is required.[1]

8.2 Before you accept instructions to act in a case you should know:

(a) the nature of the proceedings and the issues to be decided by the court;
(b) the precise nature of the issue or issues which you are to be asked to address;
(c) whether or not permission has already been given for the papers to be disclosed to you or to another expert in your field;
(d) the volume of reading which you will be required to undertake;
(e) whether or not (in an appropriate case) permission has been given for you to examine the child or children involved in the case; and whether or not it will be necessary for you to conduct interviews (and if so with whom);
(f) the time-scale within which your opinion is required;
(g) whether a date has been fixed for the hearing and whether or not you are likely to be required to give evidence.

8.3 It is of the greatest importance for the proper planning and time-tabling of a case in which you are approached to give your opinion that you should be given adequate information before agreeing to do so.

8.4 You should, in return, make clear:

(a) that the work required is within the area of your expertise;
(b) your ability to do the relevant work within a specified time scale;
(c) your availability to give evidence, in particular dates and times to avoid, and, where a hearing date has not been fixed, the amount of notice you will require to enable you conveniently to arrange a time to come to court without undue disruption to your normal clinical work.

8.5 The *Protocol*[2] also requires you to provide information about your fees. These include your hourly and global rates, your likely fee for writing your report, attending any meeting of experts and giving evidence in court. These matters are more fully addressed in Chapter 25.

8.6   As paragraph **8.5** implies, as part of your work for the court, and depending, of course, on the nature of the case and the involvement of other experts, you may be asked to attend a pre-hearing meeting of experts. This subject is covered in detail in Chapter 13. You clearly need to be given as much notice of such a meeting as possible and, whilst at the preliminary stage it is unlikely that the solicitor making enquiries will know whether or not such a meeting will be required, there is no harm in you putting down a marker to the effect that if such a meeting is called for, you should be given good notice of the fact, so that you can arrange your diary accordingly.

SUMMARY

8.7   Where your opinion is sought in a child case, you should agree to give it only if the question on which you are asked to advise is within the area of your expertise and if you are able to comply with the conditions laid down by the court for the making of your enquires and delivery of your report.

NOTES

[1]   See chapter 26 and paragraphs 2.1 and 2.2 of Appendix C to the Protocol for the manner in which enquiries should be made and the information you should provide.

[2]   See note 1.

Chapter 9

THE NATURE OF THE BRIEF
GIVEN BY THE COURT

9.1   It is very important for you to appreciate that your brief comes from the court. You must, accordingly, work to that brief. Good practice requires that the issues on which expert evidence may be required should be identified by the parties and the court at the earliest possible opportunity.[1] Thus, the need to instruct experts, the issues which they are required to address and the nature of the different disciplines required to address the relevant issues are (or should be) all debated before the court at an early directions appointment.[2]

9.2   It is, however, also very important that you should feel comfortable with the brief which you are given. There is a misconception amongst some experts that the brief is written in stone and you cannot deviate from it. This is not the case. If you cannot work to the brief given to you by the court, you should immediately say so and either refuse to act or invite the solicitor who has commissioned the report to return to the court to seek a variation in the brief. The court will pay considerable regard to a carefully expressed statement of your areas of expertise, your professional standards and your methods of work.[3]

9.3   For example, in most cases where either a physical examination or a psychiatric or psychological assessment of a child is required, the court will normally allow the child to be examined or interviewed by only one expert. This is often an expert instructed by the child's guardian or by the guardian and the other parties jointly. If one of the parties subsequently seeks a second opinion from you and if the court gives permission for a second opinion but refuses permission for you to see the child, you should only accept the brief if you feel that you can properly do the work without seeing the child.

9.4   In other cases, the court may seek advice on how a particular course of action can be put into effect, for example restarting contact between a child and an estranged parent.[4] If the brief prohibits you from considering the merits of restarting contact and if you feel that you cannot properly advise without considering that question, you should, once again, either refuse the brief or seek to have it modified.

SUMMARY

9.5   Generally speaking, you should be proactive in ensuring that:

(a) the brief you are given is appropriate;

(b) the questions on which you are asked to advise are fairly and squarely within your expertise;

(c) you are given access to all the relevant people and material necessary for the formation of your opinion;

(d) if the brief is one to which you cannot work, you should say so (giving your reasons) and either refuse to act or invite the solicitor instructing you to return to court to seek a variation.

NOTES

[1]   See Chapter 26 and paragraph 3.1 of the Protocol for the content of your letter of instruction.

[2]   See *Re G (Minors) (Expert Witnesses)* [1994] 2 FLR 291, an extract from which was set out in Appendix 3 to the first edition of this work. This aspect of case management is now also governed by the Protocol.

[3]   For some of the difficulties which can arise in this area, see Chapters 17 and 31.

[4]   For an example of a case in which an expert was instructed in order to break the deadlock in an intractable contact case, see *Re M (Contact: Long-Term Best Interests)* [2005] EWCA Civ 1090, [2006] 1 FLR 627.

Chapter 10

THE LETTER OF INSTRUCTION

10.1 Your letter of instruction is a very important document.[1] It is the practice of courts hearing family proceedings to require the letter of instruction to you to be made available to the court and to the other parties. This is part and parcel of the policy of openness which operates in family proceedings and should ensure that you are appropriately instructed.

10.2 The material to be contained in the letter of instruction is set out in paragraph 3.1 of Appendix C to the Protocol.[2] In addition, the Family Justice Council, in an appendix to its annual report, has identified a series of model questions to be posed to child mental health professionals and paediatricians in letters of instruction in proceedings under the Children Act.[3] This is also a theme in the Chief Medical Officer's Report.[4]

10.3 There is, accordingly, an ongoing debate about the form your letter of instruction should take and the material it should contain. Do not worry about this. Your task – as set out in this chapter – is to ensure that you are fully and properly instructed. That is to say:

(1) the issue or issues on which you are asked to advise are clearly articulated and within the area of your expertise;
(2) that you have all the material you need in order to carry out your enquiries and write your report; and
(3) that the time-scale within which you are being asked to report is acceptable to you.

10.4 Sometimes you will be instructed jointly by the parties and the letter of instruction to you will be agreed between their respective solicitors. This situation is covered in greater detail in Chapter 15.

10.5 Where you are instructed by one party only, the other parties will see the letter of instruction and each may, with the agreement of the other parties or the permission of the court, provide additional information or points for you to consider. None of this, of course, affects your duty to give an unbiased opinion as set out in Chapter 6.

10.6 It is essential, if you are asked to give an opinion in a child case, that you are fully instructed in relation to the area of the case on which your advice is sought. The letter of instruction should therefore always set out the context in which your opinion is sought and define carefully the specific questions you are being asked to address. If it does not do so, you should immediately seek clarification from the solicitor who commissioned the report.

10.7   It is also critically important that you only give opinions which are within the ambit of your expertise. Not only, therefore, should the letter of instruction carefully define the questions which you are being asked to address but you also have an obligation to ensure that you are happy with the ambit of the task allotted to you in the proceedings. If you feel that it is either too narrow or too wide, you should not hesitate to say so.

10.8   Careful thought should have been given to the selection of the papers to be sent to you with the letter of instruction. The letter of instruction should always list the documents which are sent. The best solicitors will send you an indexed and paginated bundle of documents which, ideally, will be the same as the bundle being used by the court. You can then cross-reference to this bundle in your report.

10.9   You will not want to spend valuable time reading through papers which are irrelevant to the opinion which you are being asked to give. On the other hand, if you venture an opinion on inadequate material, there is a substantial risk that your opinion may be unsound.

10.10   You should, therefore, not hesitate to request further information and ask for additional documentation if you think this necessary. If the documents sent to you are in any way deficient, you must say so and insist that the solicitor commissioning your report rectifies the deficiency.

10.11   You should always be allowed access to the documentation which you deem it necessary to see in order properly to conduct your enquiries.[5] If, for any reason, you are denied access to documents or material which you deem relevant to your enquiry, you should make immediate contact with the solicitor who commissioned your report. If that approach does not succeed, you should invite the solicitor to return to court to obtain an order from the judge for disclosure of the relevant documents to you.

10.12   Your letter of instruction should identify the relevant lay and professional people involved in the case and advise you of your right to talk to the other professionals engaged in it. This topic is covered in greater detail in the following chapters.

SUMMARY

10.13   It is of the utmost importance that you are properly and fully instructed and that you have access to all the material which is necessary for the proper preparation of your report. Your letter of instruction should be detailed and spell out clearly what is required of you. If it does not, or if you do not have access to material which you feel is necessary for the preparation of your report, you should not hesitate to say so and to take steps to ensure that you receive it.

NOTES

[1] The importance of the letter of instruction being tailored to the facts of the individual case and the particular task being allotted to the expert has been stressed by judges on many occasions: see, for example the judgment of Charles J in *Re R (Care: Disclosure: Nature of Proceedings)* [2002] 1 FLR 755.

[2] See Chapter 26, where Appendix C to the Protocol is set out.

[3] These questions are reproduced for reference in Appendix 2.

[4] See *Bearing Good Witness, Annex B, The Experts' Role in the Family Court*. The report was published by the Department of Health on 31 October 2006.

[5] Note, however, that you should always refer in your report to your sources and to the information which has, in particular, influenced you in reaching your conclusion. It is always very important that any such information should also have been seen by, or made available to, the parties and to their lawyers.

Chapter 11

YOUR ENQUIRIES:
THE GENERAL RULE AND SOME PITFALLS

11.1   How you go about the enquiries necessary for the writing of your report is, of course, a matter for you and, generally speaking, outside the scope of this book. You must, of course, work to the brief given to you by the court (see Chapter 9) and the court will expect you to conduct your enquiries in conformity with the highest standards of your profession and with best professional practice. That said, the court will only be concerned about your methodology if it becomes an issue in the case. You should, however, bear the following points in mind.

(1) Your report is likely to be the subject of careful scrutiny by the parties and by the court. You may be asked about the basis upon which you reached your conclusions and the material available to you. You will therefore need to be able to demonstrate that your enquiries have been both careful and thorough.

(2) You should, of course, make a careful note of all interviews which you conduct in the course of your enquiries, and you should explain in your report what factors in particular have influenced you in reaching your conclusions.

(3) If you have had clinical experience of the child or children outside the immediate ambit of the litigation (for example if you are a paediatrician who has examined or treated the child prior to proceedings being taken) you should make this clear and identify carefully the role you are being asked to play in the proceedings. As part of your preparation for giving evidence, you should liaise with the solicitor instructing you and ensure that all the relevant clinical information will be available in court. This includes (not an exhaustive list) all medical notes, hospital records, photographs, correspondence and X-rays.[1]

(5) You should always bring with you to court your file containing your notes and any original documents in your possession. You should be told in advance by the solicitor instructing you (or the lead solicitor if you are jointly instructed) what documents are in the court bundles, so that you can be sure everything you need is available. If you are not given this information, ask for it. You are the person giving evidence. You will be asked about what you have done in the case. You are likely to need to explain what you have done by reference to the written material. It is therefore very

much in your interests (as well as being very helpful to the court) that the clinical material relevant to your evidence is available, so that reference can easily be made to it.

(6) Lawyers tend to make a distinction between the functions of the treating clinician and those of the expert witness, although there is no reason in principle why a suitably qualified treating doctor should not also give expert evidence in an appropriate case. This is why, from the court's perspective, your role should be clearly defined. The distinction between the treating clinician and the expert is more fully addressed in Chapter 33.

SOME PITFALLS

11.2   The general rule, therefore, is that the court will respect the manner in which you go about your task of gathering information and writing your report. Provided you behave in a manner which is accepted by your professional body within your particular discipline, the court will not normally regard it as being its function to make suggestions to you about your methods of work, although you must, of course, be prepared to be cross-examined about them and, if necessary, to justify them.

11.3   There are, however, exceptions to the general rule. This part of this chapter will address some of them, as they have emerged in practice since the first edition of this Handbook. The importance to you of the points which have emerged warrants the inevitable element of repetition in what follows.

11.4   As is made clear in other parts of this Handbook, the key to the successful presentation of expert evidence in family proceedings is openness. You must be open about what you have done. For example, if you form your opinion on the basis of particular material such as a local authority file, fairness requires that the court and the parties should also have access to the same material in order to be able to test your conclusions.[2]

11.5   You must expect your recollection of interviews and conversations with the parties to the proceedings to be challenged. If, for example, you have not kept good notes of such interviews and conversations, you are likely to be criticised and your evidence devalued.

11.6   Equally, the court will not be impressed if, for example, you appear to have exceeded your instructions and decline for no good reason to disclose your working documents,[3] or to assist the judge on points which are plainly within your area of competence.

PRESSURE FROM THE LAWYERS REPRESENTING ONE OF THE PARTIES

11.7 It is very important that the court should perceive your report as the truly independent product of your investigation and opinion. It is, therefore, unacceptable for the lawyers representing one of the parties to the proceedings to seek to put pressure on you in order to require you to conduct your investigation in a particular way.

11.8 This form of pressure usually arises only where there is a risk that one or both parents may be prosecuted for injuries relating to the subject child or a sibling who has either died or suffered serious unexplained injuries. In such cases there is a risk that any report made by the expert will be ordered by the judge to be disclosed to the police in order to assist them in their enquiries into what is – or may be – a serious criminal offence.

11.9 This was the background to *Re AB (Care Proceedings: Disclosure of Medical Evidence to Police)*.[4] Care proceedings had been instituted in relation to a child of seven, whose two younger siblings had both died before they were a year old. The evidence pointed towards the mother being responsible for both deaths. The consultant paediatrician, instructed by the court to provide a paediatric overview for a causation hearing, wished to interview the mother as part of his investigation. She only agreed to be interviewed if the paediatrician gave four undertakings, namely (1) that he would not retain any notes of the interview; (2) that he would not reveal any answers given by the mother to any non-party to the care proceedings without the permission of the judge hearing them; (3) that he would not re-put to the mother any question to which her solicitor had taken objection; and (4) that he would limit his conclusions to the issues before the court hearing the proceedings under the Children Act. This meant that if he referred to the standard of proof, he would limit himself to the standard apposite to care proceedings. Self-evidently, the lawyers acting for the mother were attempting to protect her against the possibility of a criminal prosecution and anything she said to the paediatrician being made available to the police.

11.10 The paediatrician refused to give the first undertaking but agreed to the remaining three. In due course, an application was made for his report to be disclosed to the police and the court ordered disclosure. In so doing, it stated that advice from lawyers to their clients not to cooperate in the court's child abuse investigation was not professionally improper but was poor practice and likely to lead to an inference being drawn against the non-cooperating parent.

11.11 The principal message of the case is clear. It is not acceptable practice for lawyers representing parents to seek to put pressure on you to require you to conduct your investigation in a particular way.

11.12   In particular, it is not acceptable practice for lawyers acting for any party to put pressure on you; (1) not to retain the notes of any interviews conducted with that party; (2) not to reveal any answers given by that party to any non-party without the judge's permission; and (3) to seek to restrict the ambit or nature of the questions which you may wish to ask.

11.13   Any issue relating to the nature or extent of the expert's investigation should be referred to the court for resolution. Expert witnesses in care proceedings should not be deterred from giving the court their frank opinion by the risk that they may not have parental co-operation with their inquiries.

11.14   If you find yourself faced with a dilemma such as any of those described in this chapter, you should seek the advice of your professional body. You might also like to put the problem to the Family Justice Council for consideration.[5]

SUMMARY

11.15   Within the framework which it has laid down for your enquiries, the court will not normally seek to inhibit the manner in which you conduct your enquiries. The court will expect those enquiries to conform with the highest professional standards and best practice. You should resist any pressure sought to be imposed on you by the lawyers acting for one of the parties and which attempts to influence you either in the manner of your enquiries or your conclusions.

NOTES

[1]   This paragraph derives from the author's experience at first instance in the case of *Re M (Minors) (Care Proceedings: Conflict of Children's Wishes: Instruction of Expert Witnesses)* [1994] 1 FCR 866 in which it was only in the witness box that the expert giving evidence recalled the existence of photographs of the child's injuries which, when produced, were determinative of the case. Had the photographs been produced earlier, the case would never have proceeded to the stage it did.

[2]   See *Re L (children) (care proceedings)* [2006] EWCA Civ 1282 at paragraphs 21–22 and 66. As to an inappropriate reliance on psychometric testing see Chapter 30.

[3]   This is what happened in *Re L* (ibid). It will create real difficulties with the court if your professional body advises you that you should not disclose your working papers to the court. This is a matter which is under consideration by the Family Justice Council and if you are in any doubt about it, you should make contact with its experts committee.

[4]   [2002] EWHC 2198.

[5]   See Chapter 27.

Chapter 12

DISCUSSIONS BETWEEN EXPERTS PRIOR TO REPORTS BEING WRITTEN

12.1 The practice in family proceedings is to encourage experts instructed to advise in a case to discuss it with other experts and professionals involved in the same case.[1] Indeed, it has been said that experts instructed in a given case should always be invited to confer with each other prior to the final hearing both in order to inform their opinions and in an attempt to reach agreement or limit the issues.[2]

12.2 Contact between experts usually takes one or both of two forms:

(1) contact made between experts prior to their reports being written;
(2) a meeting of experts after reports have been completed.

12.3 There is, in some quarters, a misunderstanding of the position of experts in relation to contact with each other before reports are written. Some experts have appeared to be under the impression that they cannot talk to each other, either because the papers are confidential or because they believe their instructions prohibit informal pre-hearing discussions between experts. One of the aims of this book is to eliminate this area of misunderstanding.

12.4 Your letter of instructions should contain a paragraph to the following effect:

> 'It is expected that you will have meetings with the parents, children (*where permission is given*), social workers and the children's guardian. You are also, of course, at liberty to discuss the case with any of the other experts instructed if you feel that would assist you in writing your report. It is, however, essential both to your role as an independent expert and to the parties' perception of your independent status, that when you do have informal discussions or correspondence with any of the professionals or the lay parties involved in the case, you should make adequate note of all such discussions. You should also disclose the fact that you have had them when you write your report, and explain what influence, if any, such discussions have had upon your thinking and your conclusions.'[3]

12.5 What the court is anxious to prevent is any *unrecorded* informal discussions between particular experts which are either influential in, or determinative of, their views and to which the parties to the proceedings (including perhaps other experts) do not have access. This also applies to any documentary material to which you have access.[4]

12.6   It is therefore very important that you make an adequate note of any informal discussions you have with other experts in the case, that you set out in your report the fact that you have had such discussions and, where those discussions are influential in your conclusions, that you disclose in your report the effect they have had on your conclusions. You may be asked to produce the note of any such discussion, either in advance of the hearing or in cross-examination.

12.7   If you are in any doubt about the propriety of any discussions which you have had or wish to have with other professionals in the case, you should seek advice from the solicitor who commissioned the report from you. The basic rule, however, is that within the framework laid down for you by the court you are free to conduct your enquiries in the manner which you believe to be most compatible with reaching the right conclusion and with your own professional and ethical standards. The corollary, however, is that you should explain your methodology in your report. You must also be able to defend it in court.

SUMMARY

12.8   In making your enquiries for the purpose of your report, you are free to talk to other professionals in the case. You should, however, make a note of any such discussions, and refer to them in your report. If any such discussion has been influential in reaching your conclusion, you should say so in your report.

NOTES

[1]   See the fourth and fifth bullet points in paragraph 3.1 of Appendix C to the Protocol set out in Chapter 26.

[2]   *Re S (Child Abuse Cases: Management)* [1992] 1 FCR 31; *Re C (Expert Evidence: Disclosure: Practice)* [1995] 1 FLR 204.

[3]   This paragraph is slightly different from the letter set out in the *Handbook of Best Practice in Children Act Cases* Children Act Advisory Committee (DOH, June 1997). The reason for this was that in *Re CB and JB (Care Proceedings: Guidelines)* [1998] 2 FLR 211, the author found that the version set out in the Handbook of Best Practice had been read by one of the experts in that case as prohibiting such discussions. The Expert Witness Group also produced a draft letter of instruction for expert witnesses in children proceedings, which represents good practice. It reads as follows:

'**Contact with others**

You may wish to contact the solicitors of the other parties or the [parents] [carers] direct, to arrange meetings or for other practical reasons. Please fell free to do so. However, if in your contact with the solicitors you discuss any matter of relevance, please inform us promptly and let us have copies of any reports or information given to you. **Please keep a careful record of all pertinent discussions with other experts or parties.** For ease of reference here are the names, addresses and telephone numbers of the most important contacts [add whenever two or more experts are being instructed: including in particular other expert[s] who have been instructed to consider the same issues. You may be required to attend a meeting with the[se] other expert[s] in order to establish agreed facts, common findings and areas of disagreement.]' (bold emphasis added).

[4]   It is a necessary part of the forensic process in children's cases that parents should be able to mount a proper challenge to the conclusions reached by local authorities and expert witness. Thus if an expert witness reaches a conclusion based in whole or in part on material to which the parents have not had access, the court is likely to deem the proceedings unfair and may well hesitate before placing reliance on the expert's opinion. For a recent example of this, see *Re L (Children) (Care Proceedings)* [2006] EWCA (Civ) 1282; [2006] 3 FCR 301 (25 August 2006).

Chapter 13

MEETINGS OF EXPERTS
DIRECTED BY THE COURT

13.1 Meetings of experts arranged as a consequence of directions from the court are an important element in the process of preparation for a hearing, and detailed provision for them is made in paragraphs 5.1 to 5.3 of Appendix C to the Protocol.[1] At the same time, the obvious needs to be stated. Simply because there are experts in the case does not mean that a pre-hearing face-to-face meeting of experts is necessary.

13.2 Like every other area of good practice, where meetings of experts are:

(a) necessary;
(b) set up with care; and
(c) conducted with intellectual rigour and discipline,

they can save an enormous amount of court time and reduce the costs of a case substantially. Where, however, such meetings are unfocused or badly conducted, they can obfuscate rather than clarify issues, thereby lengthening a case and increasing costs.

13.3 A meeting of experts is necessary only if there is something for you to discuss. If, on paper, you are all agreed and there is nothing in your reports which requires elucidation or amplification, there should be no need for you to meet and there should be no need for you to attend court to give oral evidence. If, therefore you find that you have been summoned to give oral evidence after a meeting at which you understood that the issues arising from your report had been agreed, you should, in advance, query the reason for your attendance. If, despite this, you are nonetheless required to attend unnecessarily (as you perceive it) you should take the opportunity during the course of your evidence to enquire of the judge why you have been summoned, alternatively to point out politely to the judge that you do not think it necessary for you to have attended. You must appreciate, however, that your report has been written in a forensic context. Thus the fact that all the experts are agreed that an injury is non-accidental does not mean that the suspected perpetrator or perpetrators will accept their opinion. In these circumstances, the right to a fair trial may require one or more of the experts to attend, so that their opinions can formally be challenged.[2]

13.4   A meeting of experts is usually required, either because it is necessary to attempt to define or limit areas of disagreement, or because there are points in the case which require elucidation. The first question, therefore, is whether or not in such a case it is necessary for you to meet face to face.

13.5   In difficult child cases the experts are often widely geographically located. The courts recognise that it will not always be reasonable to expect you to find time to travel long distances in order to meet face to face. In many cases, you can agree or limit the areas of disagreement by telephone or fax. Sometimes telephone conferencing is sufficient and serious consideration should be given to telephone conferencing in every case, provided always that any such conference has a proper agenda, is called to answer specific questions and is competently chaired and minuted.[3]

13.6   Where a face-to-face meeting is arranged, sufficient time should be set aside for it so that the discussion does not take place under undue pressure of time. Equally, the meeting should not take place at the last minute but should be time-tabled so as to enable the parties to have the opportunity to discuss the outcome and for the experts to reschedule their diaries if agreement is reached and they are not required to give evidence.

WHICH EXPERTS SHOULD ATTEND A MEETING?

13.7   In many cases, the essential issue is a factual one: for example, was the injury to the child accidental or non-accidental? If the latter, what was the mechanism and timing? What degree of force was required? In such cases, the expert evidence relevant to its elucidation is usually medical and goes to causation and timing. In these circumstances, it is rarely helpful for such a meeting to be attended by psychologists and psychiatrists.

13.8   Lawyers seeking to organise a meeting of experts need always to give thought to the subject matter to be addressed by the particular meeting and the relevance of the disciplines of those invited to attend. This is a matter in which you plainly have a legitimate interest. If you think that a meeting is unnecessary, either because there is no issue between your colleagues and yourself, or because you think it unlikely to produce agreement or even a narrowing of the issues, you should explain your view to your colleagues and to the solicitor who commissioned your report.

13.9   A global meeting of experts from different disciplines may sometimes be appropriate if all the issues in a case are up for discussion and resolution. Such a situation is, however, in my experience, unusual.

13.10   Not only must great care be taken to ensure that experts' meetings are properly constituted to meet their particular objective, care must also be taken to ensure that, if separate meetings of different disciplines do take place in the context of a given case, those meetings are complementary to each other and have the same objective, namely the elucidation and, if possible, resolution of the relevant medical issues in the case.

13.11 It is therefore very important that you tell the solicitor who commissioned your report if you feel a meeting is unnecessary or that it is being called to address the wrong issues.

13.12 As part of the non-adversarial nature of the proceedings, the collection and marshalling of expert evidence in cases relating to children should be a co-operative process between the lawyers and the experts involved, irrespective of the source of their instructions. The issues in the case which require expert evidence must be identified and discussed in advance of the hearing. If agreement in relation to them is impossible, oral evidence will have to be called and tested and the judge will need to rule.

13.13 The object of experts' meetings, therefore, is to reduce or eliminate the need for contested oral expert evidence. This is often not sufficiently appreciated.

THE CONDUCT OF THE MEETING

13.14 If meetings of experts are to succeed in achieving their objective of eliminating or narrowing areas of disagreement, it is essential that a strict intellectual discipline is applied to them. Meetings must therefore be focused carefully and clearly on the issues which you are to address.

13.15 Furthermore, the questions posed for you to answer must be clear and as straightforward as the subject matter allows. Prolixity is to be avoided. There is no point in asking experts to address 100 questions if the subject matter can sensibly be covered by 10 or fewer. Ultimately, the questions to be addressed are a matter for the lawyers in the case and the judge. The bullet points set out in paragraph 5.2 of Appendix C to the Protocol[4] should ensure that good sense prevails. This provides that the agenda for the meeting (and the list of questions) should be given to you seven days prior to the meeting. This should give you some time to query the agenda and the questions with your colleagues and with the agenda's author.

13.16 The format of an experts' meeting must ultimately be a matter for those attending it. However, there are certain basic guidelines which should always be observed.

13.17 There must be a clear agenda for the meeting. Specific questions for you to answer, or propositions for you to address, must be drawn up by the lawyers and presented to the meeting. The questions should be as concise and as clear as possible. As the Protocol now requires, they must be agreed between the parties' lawyers and given to the experts who are to attend the meeting in good time to enable you to prepare for it.

13.18   Because meetings of experts are perceived by the courts as a forensic tool whereby medical evidence addresses issues which are relevant to the court's decision, courts tend to the view that the meetings of experts which are most productive are those chaired by a lawyer.

13.19   The obvious choice for this role is the solicitor or counsel instructed by the children's guardian. Either of those lawyers should have a clear and unpartisan view of the issues in the case. It should, thus, normally be their responsibility to ensure that the agenda for the meeting addresses the issues upon which agreement is being sought or in respect of which the areas of agreement and disagreement need to be defined.

13.20   However, if lawyers are to chair meetings of experts, they must be sensitive to the different areas of expertise present at the meeting, and must ensure that they understand the weight which the doctors themselves give to each speciality. In a case involving complex medical issues, it may be sensible for the meeting to be chaired jointly by the child's lawyer and one of the doctors.

13.21   The court expects the lawyers for all of the parties to direct their minds to the questions which are to be posed to you. As has already been twice stated, the questions should be as simple and as straightforward as the subject-matter allows. It is for the lawyers and, in particular, in the preparation for a meeting of experts, for the solicitor or counsel instructed by the children's guardian to distil the relevant issues in the case into a series of straightforward questions or propositions.

13.22   Ultimately, of course, if agreement cannot be reached as to the questions to be asked of the experts, the court will have to set the agenda. It should, however, normally be quite unnecessary to involve the court in this process.

13.23   Meetings of experts should be planned as a co-operative exercise between the lawyers and yourselves. The importance of your role in any such meeting is self-evident. You will therefore be asked to co-operate in making yourselves available for and participating in such meetings. If, however, you feel that a meeting is unnecessary, or had been called to address the wrong issues, or that the wrong disciplines have been invited, or that it is unlikely to achieve its objective, you should say so.

SHOULD THE LAWYERS FOR THE PARTIES ATTEND?

13.24   In my view the answer to this question should usually be 'no'. The meeting of experts is an evidence gathering tool. It is not an adversarial mini-trial. The parties' lawyers will, inevitably, be partisan. They are unlikely to sit as silent observers of the process, and the temptation to cross-examine or ask additional questions is unlikely to be resisted. In addition, it is likely that you will feel less comfortable in exchanging frank opinions with your colleagues in the presence of the parties' lawyers, and the whole purpose of the meeting may be frustrated.

13.25   It is important to remember that the meeting is part of the evidence gathering process and cannot therefore be 'off the record'. You should not express views at the meeting which you are not prepared to express in court. At the same time, the purpose of the meeting is to discuss the relevant issues and to narrow points of disagreement if they cannot be eliminated. There needs, therefore, to be a frank and open dialogue.

MINUTES AND STATEMENTS OF AGREEMENT AND DISAGREEMENT

13.26   The view expressed in paragraph **13.24**, however, makes it all the more important that a proper record is kept of all meetings of experts. This is usually best done by the children's guardian although, in complex cases, it may be appropriate to employ a shorthand writer. Whether or not to have a verbatim transcript should be a matter of prior discussion and agreement and, if necessary, should be referred to the judge to whom the case has been allocated. Transcripts are expensive and the need to have one would have to be justified by the particular facts and complexities of the case.

13.27   The reasons why a proper record of the meeting is important are, I think, self-evident. The judge may have to hear evidence about what was and what was not said at the meeting, although the purpose of the meeting, if properly conducted, is to eliminate or reduce the need for oral evidence on disputed medical issues. The advantage of a verbatim transcript is that it should eliminate any dispute about what was said. A particular disadvantage is that, unless properly controlled by the judge at the subsequent hearing, it proffers a basis for cross-examination of the experts in which the issues in the case become submerged in an arid argument about what individual doctors meant when they were recorded as having made a particular remark.

13.28   As with most procedural tools, experts' meetings work best when they are competently arranged and conducted and when all their participants fix their minds on the real objective of the meeting. Thus, the most important aspect of the meeting is that its contents are promptly distilled into a schedule of points of agreement and disagreement. This will be a document to which you can put your name and which thus acquires evidential status. Such a statement will be given to the judge who will have read it before you give evidence (assuming oral evidence is still necessary).

SUMMARY

13.29   Meetings of experts pursuant to a direction from the court are an important forensic tool. They can save much time, by narrowing issues or by reaching agreement thereby rendering the oral evidence of experts unnecessary. However, a strict intellectual discipline must be applied to them. Whilst the logistics of setting up, conducting and reporting on such meetings are largely matters for the lawyers, experts have a vital role in ensuring that meetings are set up only when they are necessary and that they are productive. For their success, they depend upon the manner in which they are set up and conducted and upon all the participants in them focusing upon achieving a clear outcome. Their principal objective is to achieve a clear statement of points of agreement and disagreement and thus to limit or eliminate the need for oral expert evidence at the hearing of the case.

NOTES

[1]   See Chapter 26. This chapter deals with meetings of experts designed to deal with evidential issues. You should be aware that, following the second conference organised by the President of the Family Division's Interdisciplinary Committee (published as *Divided Duties* (Family Law, 1998)), a practice has developed in care proceedings whereby the court sometimes directs a meeting of relevant professionals to discuss the local authority's care plan. You may also be invited to such a meeting – although this is unlikely – but if you are invited to such a meeting, you should consider carefully with the solicitor instructing you whether or not it would be appropriate for you to attend. For the approach of the Protocol to such meetings see paragraph 5.4, set out in Chapter 26.

[2]   There are also occasions, albeit very rare, in which the apparent medical consensus is either not a true consensus or is wrong: see *W v Oldham MBC* [2005] EWCA Civ 1247 and [2007] EWHC 136 (Fam) discussed in Chapter 32.

[3]   Consideration should also be given to the possibility of video conferencing if the facility is available. It is to be hoped that in the future it may be possible for doctors to give evidence in this way, particularly if the facility is available in the hospital in which they work.

[4]   See Chapter 26.

Chapter 14

PRE-HEARING CONFERENCES WITH COUNSEL AND/OR WITH THE SOLICITOR WHO HAS COMMISSIONED THE EXPERT REPORT

14.1 If you have been instructed by only one of the parties, there is nothing improper or inappropriate about being asked to attend a pre-hearing conference with counsel and/or the solicitor who has the conduct of that party's case in court. The purpose of that conference is to clarify and discuss your report; to bring you up to date with events in the case and to discuss with you any material which has emerged since you wrote your report, notably perhaps, a report by one of your colleagues.

14.2 It is, however, bad practice in proceedings relating to children, bordering on professional impropriety, for lawyers to seek to 'coach' experts or to invite you to form or modify particular opinions because they favour their client's case. If you are approached in this way, not only should your resist the approach firmly but you should consider making a complaint to the High Court Family Division Liaison Judge for the circuit concerned (see Chapter 24 and Appendix 4) or to the professional body of the lawyers concerned. Such behaviour on the part of family lawyers cuts across the whole ethos of the independence of the expert and the philosophy underlying the purpose of expert evidence in family proceedings.

14.3 You must be free to express opinions relevant to the child's welfare in a wholly disinterested way and without partisan pressure from lawyers.

14.4 Seeking to identify areas of agreement and disagreement in readiness for a court hearing should not be regarded as 'drawing battle lines'. Thus the meetings of experts described in the Chapter 13 are a forensic tool but gathering expert evidence is not to be regarded as an 'adversarial' process, rather as a co-operative exercise.

14.5 Difficulties may arise in cases in which parents whose children are the subject of care proceedings also face (or fear facing) arrest and prosecution for a serious criminal offence if they are frank with you in the course of your enquiries. This particular dilemma is addressed in Chapter 11.

SUMMARY

14.6   There is nothing improper or inappropriate about you attending a pre-hearing conference with counsel and with the solicitor instructing you in a particular case. However, any attempt by lawyers to interfere with your independence or to persuade you to tailor your views to a particular standpoint is to be both deprecated and resisted.

Chapter 15

JOINT INSTRUCTIONS

15.1 It is quite common for individual experts in family proceedings to be jointly instructed by the parties to the proceedings. In care proceedings, this usually means that you will be instructed jointly by the solicitor acting for the child, the local authority solicitor and the parents' solicitor(s). The solicitor from whom you receive your letter of instruction will be the 'lead' solicitor for this purpose and will usually be the solicitor instructed by the children's guardian on behalf of the child.

15.2 Apart from ensuring that you receive your letter of instruction and all the relevant documents, many of the principal functions of the lead solicitor in a case of joint instruction are largely administrative. One important task is to liaise with the other solicitors in the case; another is to ensure that all the solicitors in the case receive copies of all the correspondence which is generated as a consequence of your involvement.

15.3 The lead solicitor should be your first port of call if you require further documentation or information or if you have a problem or query.

15.4 The lead solicitor should also be responsible for keeping you up to date with developments in the case and for making the arrangements for any meeting of experts or professionals which you are invited to attend.

15.5 The lead solicitor will be responsible for ensuring, if you have to give oral evidence, that your evidence is time-tabled for a date and time which is convenient for you. The lead solicitor will also be responsible for ensuring that you are paid (see Chapter 25).

REASONS FOR JOINT INSTRUCTION

15.6 There may be a number of reasons why the court has ordered a report from a single, jointly instructed expert. It may be, for example, that an intimate examination of the child in the case is required, or the court wants a psychiatrist to interview and assess the child. Courts are always anxious to limit the number of physical or psychiatric examinations which a child has to undergo, and so may permit only a single examination by one expert for the purposes of the case.

15.7 Another example of joint instruction is where a paediatric or psychiatric overview of the case is required. A third situation is where a discrete scientific issue arises, such as a hair or blood test for drugs, where joint instruction enables the cost of the exercise to be shared between the parties.

15.8 Joint instructions can, however, pose difficulties both for the expert instructed and for the lawyers in the case. This chapter will examine the benefits of joint instruction and some of the problems which arise.

THE ADVANTAGES OF THE JOINTLY INSTRUCTED EXPERT

15.9 The fact that you have been jointly instructed means that you have either been chosen jointly by, or at the very least are acceptable to, all the parties in the case. The process of joint instruction should thus tend to exclude from the legal process experts with views which tend strongly to favour one particular point of view. Furthermore, where the opinion of a jointly instructed expert is sufficiently authoritative and is accepted by the parties and the court, a great deal of court time and a large amount of legal costs can be saved.

15.10 If properly carried through, the joint instruction of a single expert may reduce the delay in the case being heard. There are, however, cases in which a party who disagrees with the conclusions of the jointly instructed expert (usually one or both of the child's parents) may be able to make out a case for a second opinion. Cases in which an expert is instructed jointly need therefore to be time-tabled with this possibility in mind so that, if a second opinion is required, there is time for it to be obtained without postponing the date fixed for the final hearing.[1]

THE DISADVANTAGES OF JOINT INSTRUCTION

15.11 To be the sole, jointly instructed expert in a difficult case places a considerable burden of responsibility on the expert concerned. The point on which you are being asked to advise may, you feel, be determinative of the child's future, yet there is nobody against whose opinion your diagnosis can be tested or with whom the burden of decision-making can be shared. You do not have a colleague from the same or a similar discipline instructed in the case with whom you can discuss your views. Your work is thus not the subject of peer review.

15.12 Although the burden of responsibility is substantial, you should remember that you do not decide the case: that is the judge's task. None the less, you should agree to accept a joint instruction only if you are wholly confident of your ability to undertake the brief given to you by the court.

15.13 As explained in paragraph **15.10**, joint instruction can create difficulty and delay if the opinion of the jointly instructed expert is challenged by one of the parties who then wish to seek a second opinion. If this happens, then, depending of course of the facts of the particular case, you should not regard it as an affront to your expertise. In a very difficult child case, a second opinion is often very helpful to the court. It may also be helpful to you. If there is agreement, the chances of the correct solution for the child are increased: if there is disagreement, the issues can be fully and properly debated.

15.14 The legal status of the jointly instructed expert is not always clear. Whilst this is primarily a matter for the lawyers to discuss and agree amongst themselves, questions arise as to the extent to which it is proper for the jointly instructed expert to attend conferences with the lawyers for the individual parties, or to discuss the case with them. Difficulties can also arise in relation to the extent to which a jointly instructed expert can be challenged by way of cross-examination in the absence of any second opinion giving a different view.

15.15 The normal rule is that where your report is provided following instructions from the solicitors for one of the parties, you are called to give evidence by the lawyer acting for the party who commissioned your report. You are then cross-examined by the lawyers for the other parties to the case (including the lawyer instructed on behalf of the child) and re-examined by the lawyer for the party who commissioned your report. This is explained in greater detail in Chapter 23.

15.16 However, if you are jointly instructed, several things can happen. If your conclusions are accepted by the lead solicitor's team, the likelihood is that you will be called by the lead solicitor or his or her barrister, and cross-examined by the other lawyers in the normal way. If, however, your report is not accepted in this way, the likelihood is that the judge will intervene and call you as a witness of the court. This will enable all the lawyers to cross-examine you – that is to say to challenge your opinion by asking you leading questions adapted to their particular client's point of view.[2]

15.17 Sometimes you will write a report on a single instruction which contradicts the case being advanced by the party who commissioned your report. In this case, as explained in Chapter 3, your report must be produced, but the party who commissioned it may well not want to call you as a witness. In these circumstances, if your oral evidence is still required, one of two things is likely to happen. Either you will be called by the lawyers for one of the other parties and the lawyer for the party who commissioned your report will be allowed to cross-examine you, or alternatively, the judge will formally call you as a witness of the court and permit all the parties to cross-examine.

15.18 If all this seems a bit hard on you, the legal justification for it is to be found in the need for the hearing to be fair; or to put the matter in ECHR terms, Article 6 compliant.[3] Thus, for example, parents who are likely to lose their child to a care order must be given the opportunity fully to test the evidence on which the local authority (and, where relevant, the children's guardian) relies. This can only be achieved under the present system by cross-examination.[4]

15.19   Lay parties who commission an expert's report frequently see its purpose in terms of obtaining an opinion which is favourable to them. They may have similar expectations of a jointly instructed expert. That is why the role of the sole, jointly appointed expert is so important.

GUIDELINES FOR THE JOINTLY INSTRUCTED EXPERT WITNESS

15.20   All the duties set out in Chapter 6 continue to apply to the jointly instructed expert witness. Subject to the terms of the brief given to you by the court, you have similar autonomy over the way you conduct your enquiries. The particular watchwords for the jointly instructed expert, however, are openness and even-handed communication.

15.21   Difficulties can particularly arise once you have written your report. What, for example, is the position if one party wishes to discuss your report with you, or wishes you to attend a conference without the other parties being present? Who can you talk to in the case about your report?

15.22   There remains no guidance from the courts on these questions. However, some points are reasonably clear. The first is that you will, at all times, exercise your professional and clinical judgment and behave in conformity with the ethical guidelines of your own professional body. This should not be difficult.

15.23   This leaves the question of your contact with the lawyers for the various parties. It is particularly in this area that difficulties can arise.

15.24   It is very important that the jointly instructed expert should not be perceived by any one of the parties as part of an opposing team. It is also very important for you to remember that the only documents or conversations in proceedings relating to children which are absolutely confidential and in respect of which disclosure cannot be ordered are those which cover the legal advice which the parties receive from their lawyers. This is called 'legal professional privilege'.

15.25   What is said to you during the course of your investigations, and what you say to others, is not covered by legal professional privilege. As a jointly instructed expert, it is simply not possible for you to have confidential discussions with one of the parties, the existence of which are not disclosed and the content of which are not recorded. In other words, where you are an expert witness in a child case there is no such thing as an 'off the record' or 'without prejudice' conversation.

PRACTICAL IMPLICATIONS OF JOINT INSTRUCTION

15.26   There is nothing wrong, in principle, with a jointly instructed expert having conversations or meetings with the lawyers for one party, provided the fact of such contact and its content are made known to the other parties. Much will depend on the facts of the individual case and the manner in which you feel it appropriate to address the questions on which you are asked to advise.

15.27   You may, for example, think it inappropriate in a particular case to attend a conference with counsel for one of the parties. On the other hand, in another case you make take the view, after you have written your report, that it is necessary to have discussions with the parties or with their solicitors individually or to talk through your conclusions with the parents with their solicitor present.

15.28   If you decide that conversations such as those described in the paragraph **15.27** are appropriate, you should not hesitate to arrange them. You must, however, ensure that everything is done in the open and is transparent. Thus, both the fact that you have had such discussions and, if relevant, their content and outcome must be made known to the other parties and to the court.

15.29   Equally, in a particular case you may feel (and are entitled to require) that all queries arising out of your report should be raised with you and be dealt with by you in writing so that you can be confident that each of the parties has received the same information contained in the same document. This is sometimes the safest course and the one most likely to avoid misunderstandings and misinterpretation. If this is the approach you prefer, it is one for which you cannot be criticised.

15.30   The dangers of conversations between experts and lawyers outside the courtroom itself are self-evident. You run the risk of being misrepresented or misunderstood. You also run the risk of giving the appearance of partiality. You lay yourself open to the suggestion that you have been inconsistent and cross-examination along the lines of:

> 'when you spoke to the parents' solicitor on the telephone, you said something quite different; you told them so and so, didn't you?'

15.31   You obviously do not want to put yourself in a position where your independence and professional integrity can be called into question or from which misunderstandings may arise. Equally, you do not want to be accused of inconsistency or of giving one message to one party and a different message to another.

15.32   You may consider it appropriate to arrange a meeting with all the parties' legal representatives to discuss your report and your conclusions. The advantage of this is that it provides a forum for questions and discussion in keeping with the inquisitorial role of the jointly instructed expert whose duty is to the child and to the court. Furthermore, it provides an opportunity for you, as the jointly instructed expert, to express your views on the validity, wisdom or otherwise of a second opinion being sought to test any of the conclusions you may have reached.

15.33   If you consider that a meeting such as that described in paragraph **15.32** is appropriate and may be of value, whether or not it has been suggested by any of the legal advisers, you should invite the lead solicitor to make the arrangements.

15.34   It is, of course, quite improper for the lawyers for any party to seek to put pressure on you to change your opinion. This issue is identified in Chapter 11. If, as the jointly instructed expert, you feel that is happening you should say so. It is not, however, improper for lawyers to put points to you which they feel you have overlooked or misinterpreted or for them to invite you to reconsider your opinion in the light of fresh material. There is a clear distinction between these approaches.

15.35   If you do engage in correspondence with individual lawyers in the case, make sure that the lead solicitor arranges for your letters to be copied to the other parties (see paragraph **15.2**).

15.36   If you have a telephone conversation with one of the parties' solicitors, you should make a written note of it as soon as possible. Alternatively, since competent solicitors always make what they call an 'attendance note' of all relevant conversations they have during the conduct of a case, you can ask the solicitor to send you a copy of the attendance note made of any conversation with you. If this is done and you disagree with the note, you should write at once to the solicitor in question, putting the record straight.

WHAT TO DO IF YOU ARE UNHAPPY

15.37   If you are uneasy about a particular course of action which is proposed, or about attending a particular meeting, or having a particular conversation or discussion, the best course is, probably, not to do it. Alternatively, speak or write to the lead solicitors and ask their advice. If necessary, get that solicitor to obtain agreement for what you want to do from the other lawyers in the case. If what you want to do is controversial and of enough importance, ask the child's solicitor to set up a directions appointment before the judge, so that the judge can rule on the point.

15.38   Always remember that your function is to advise the court, not the parties. In a disputed case, the proper forum for the discussion of your report is the courtroom. The person with whom you are discussing the case outside the courtroom may later be cross-examining you on your report in the courtroom.

That is not easy either for the lawyer or for you and is another reason why you should be very cautious about having out of court discussions with the lawyers in the case apart from the lead solicitor.

SUMMARY

15.39   Being a jointly instructed expert places a particularly heavy burden on you. Follow your professional judgment in making your enquiries. Be open and even handed in your dealings with the lawyers. Make a written note of any conversations you have with them. If the lawyers wish to discuss your report with you in advance of the hearing or if you feel that you should, for example, take the opportunity to explain your conclusions to the parents with their lawyers present, you should feel free to do so. An alternative may be to invite all the lawyers in the case to a meeting at which you can explain your conclusions and answer questions. If you do have a conference with one of the parties and their lawyers, you must be able to justify the need for such a conference. You should ensure that the other parties know you are doing it and that a proper record of what you say at the conference is made.

NOTES

[1]   For an illustration of the difficulties which can arise when you are the jointly appointed sole expert, see Chapter 32.

[2]   For the nature and purpose of cross-examination see Chapter 23.

[3]   For a discussion of ECHR Article 6 see Chapter 28.

[4]   This topic is further discussed in Chapter 23.

Chapter 16

WHERE THERE ARE BOTH CRIMINAL AND CARE PROCEEDINGS UNDER THE CHILDREN ACT 1989

16.1 If you are a paediatrician, a radiologist or a pathologist, you may find yourself involved in a case in which parents are facing criminal proceedings relating to a dead or seriously injured child, whilst the surviving siblings or the injured child are concurrently the subject of care proceedings under the Children Act 1989.

16.2 Similarly, in a private law case[1] between parents where the issue is residence or contact, there may be an ongoing police/social services investigation into allegations of abuse against one or both of the parents.

16.3 There is, of course, no reason why you should not make a statement to the police as well as writing a report for the care proceedings. Indeed, it is your duty to assist the police in their enquiries if you have medical information which is relevant to the injuries suffered by a child.

16.4 If, however, you have been instructed in the care proceedings, you are not at liberty to disclose your report in those proceedings to the police without the permission of the court hearing the care proceedings. This is because that report is confidential to those proceedings and cannot, without the permission of the court, be shown to any person or body not engaged in those proceedings. The same rule also applies to any documents prepared for the purposes of the proceedings and filed with the court.

16.5 There is one very clear distinction between reports by experts written in proceedings under the Children Act and reports written for the purposes of criminal proceedings. In the latter, the person who has commissioned the report is entitled to claim what is known as legal professional privilege for the report. That means that they cannot be compelled to reveal what has passed between the client and their legal advisers. This privilege extends to experts' reports written in criminal proceedings. So, where a father was facing criminal charges relating to children who were the subject of care proceedings, he could not be compelled in the care proceedings to disclose either the identity of any expert instructed in the criminal proceedings or that expert's report.[2]

16.6   As is made clear in earlier chapters, however, whilst your report is confidential to the court, all relevant information obtained during the course of your enquiries must be shared in your report with the other parties and the court.

ACCEPTING INSTRUCTIONS IN BOTH SETS OF PROCEEDINGS

16.7   If you are jointly instructed by the solicitors for the children's guardian, the parents and the local authority to advise the court in care proceedings, you should think very carefully before either making a statement to the police or accepting instructions on behalf of the defence in any concurrent criminal proceedings. The reason for this is that your information about the case will have come from the confidential material assembled for the care proceedings and your position as an independent expert in those proceedings may be compromised if you become actively involved in the criminal proceedings.

16.8   At the same time if, during the course of your enquiries in the care proceedings you come across material which you believe to be of importance either to the prosecution or to the defence or if, having completed your enquiries, you feel that your report should be seen by either the prosecution or the defence in the criminal proceedings, you should advise the solicitor who commissioned your report (the solicitor instructed by the children's guardian in the example given). It will then be for that solicitor to apply to the court in order to obtain the leave of the judge in charge of the care proceedings for your report or the relevant information to be disclosed.

INFORMATION ACQUIRED DURING THE COURSE OF THE PROCEEDINGS WHICH REQUIRES IMMEDIATE ACTION

16.9   However, if during the course of your enquiries in care proceedings you come across child protection information which, in your judgment, requires immediate action on your part (such as reporting that information to the police or to social services), you should not hesitate to do so.[3]

SUMMARY

16.10   There is no reason why you should not make statements both to the police and in the care proceedings under the Children Act. However, knowledge acquired as a result of your instruction in the care proceedings, or any report you write in those proceedings, can only be disclosed to the prosecution or to the defence with the leave of the court hearing the Children Act proceedings.

NOTES

[1]   For the distinction between private and public law proceedings relating to children see Chapter 3.

[2]   *S County Council v B* [2000] 2 FLR 161 (Charles J). Legal professional privilege also applies in cases under the Children Act 1989 to the extent that legal advisers cannot be compelled to reveal what their clients have said to them. However, as made clear in Chapter 4, litigation privilege does not apply to experts' reports filed in proceedings under the Children Act.

[3]   See *Re M (a Child) (Children and Family Reporter) (Disclosure)* [2002] EWCA Civ 1199, [2003] Fam 26, a case which related to child protection information received by the CAFCASS Children and Family Reporter (CFR) in private law proceedings and in which the Court of Appeal decided that the CFRs did not need the court's permission to disclose to the police and social services information about the child acquired in the course of their inquiries which, in their professional judgment, raised child protection issues. Plainly, the same principle applies with even greater force to medical experts who receive such information during the course of their enquiries irrespective of the nature of the proceedings in which the information is acquired.

Chapter 17

WRITING THE REPORT

17.1 There is no specific format required by the court for an expert's report.[1] The following suggestions touch only on topics which are particularly helpful to the court.

17.2 It is important that you give a full curriculum vitae which explains the basis upon which you have the expertise to address the issues contained in the report. This can, for example, be done by appending your CV to the report and by a reference to it in the text of the report.[2]

17.3 Although the initial documents sent to you will have been listed in your letter of instruction, it is important that you should identify in your report all the documents you have seen. Either list them (perhaps in an appendix to the report) or attach a copy of the letter of instruction to your report and, in the body of that report, list any additional documents which you have considered.

17.4 It is also important that you should set out in summary form all the enquiries you have made. This will, of course, include any interviews you have conducted and any other material, such as videos, which you have seen. It will also include discussions with fellow experts and other professionals if these have occurred.

17.5 The court looks above all for clarity in presentation and in the conclusions reached. The court is concerned with:

(1) the issues it asked you to address;
(2) the material you have considered;
(3) the conclusions you have reached; and
(4) your reasons for reaching those conclusions.

17.6 Try to keep your report to a manageable length. Put yourself in the position of the judge who is reading your report for the first time and who is interested in the matters set out in the preceding paragraph. If you need to set out the detail of interviews or material upon which your conclusions are based, put them in an appendix.

17.7 Your conclusions should, wherever possible, be clear and logically argued with the reasoning for them fully explained. Plain English should be used wherever possible and complex or unusual medical terms explained. Use of double spacing, pagination, short, numbered paragraphs and sub-headings all make for easy reading. Also, write only on one side of each sheet of paper. Your report will be photocopied many times and one of the easiest mistakes made in photocopying is for only one side of the page to be copied.

17.8 If, after writing your report, fresh information is made available to you, you must inform the commissioning solicitor in writing of any change which that information requires in your report. This should be done in a form which can be made available to the other parties and the court.

17.9 If you take the view that you have not had access to sufficient material to express a full opinion, you must say so in your report.

17.10 It is very important that you address the specific issues which you are asked to address and that you do not deviate into areas outside your expertise. If, however, you have not been asked to express an opinion on an issue which you feel is relevant and it is one on which you can properly express an opinion, you should do so. Some letters of instruction will give you the opportunity to comment on 'any other issue which you feel to be relevant'.

17.11 At the same time, you should not feel the need to reach a particular conclusion simply for the sake of doing so. If, having conducted your enquiries, you remain uncertain about the point on which you have been asked to advise, or simply do not know the answer to it, you should not hesitate to say so. The court wants your honest, professional opinion, not a hypothesis or an argument.

SUMMARY

17.12 There is no particular format for your report required by the court. It should, however, be written in plain English. It should address all the issues on which you have been asked to advise. Your report should be clear and well argued. It should identify all the material you have considered and relied upon. Its conclusions should also be clear and well reasoned.

NOTES

1   Useful guidelines for the structure of an expert's report are to be found in *the Expert Witness Pack* (see attached CD-ROM) and in Tufnell 'Psychiatric Court Reports in Child Care Cases: What Constitutes Good Practice' published in the *Association of Child Psychology and Psychiatry Review and Newsletter* (1993) vol 15, pp 219–24. There is also an excellent chapter and model report by Dr Frank Bamford in *Recent Advances in Paediatrics*, vol 12, ed TJ David (Churchill Livingston, 1994). See also David, TJ, *Avoidable pitfalls when writing medical reports for court proceedings in cases of suspected child abuse*, Archives of Disease in Childhood 2004; 89; 799–804, and the suggested reading list in Appendix 1, particularly Plotnikoff and Woolfson *Reporting to Court under the Children Act (A Handbook for Social Services)* (DOH, 1996).

2   Following the decision of the Court of Appeal in *Toth v Jarman* [2006] EWCA Civ 1028 (19 July 2006), you should also say whether or not you believe there is any conflict of interest arising from your report and if you think such a conflict exists you should disclose it, even if you think it wholly irrelevant. If you do identify such a conflict, it will be sensible to explain in brief terms why you think it irrelevant: see the judgment of the court at paragraph 100 et seq, and in particular at paragraph 120 where it said:

> Without wishing to be over-prescriptive or to limit consideration by the Civil Procedure Rules Committee, we are of the view that consideration should be given to requiring an expert to make a statement at the end of his report on the following lines:
>
> (1)   that he has no conflict of interest of any kind, other than any which he has disclosed in his report;
>
> (2)   that he does not consider that any interest which he has disclosed affects his suitability as an expert witness on any issue on which he has given evidence;
>
> (3)   that he will advise the party by whom he is instructed if, between the date of his report and the trial, there is any change in circumstances which affects his answers to (a) or (b) above.

Chapter 18

CHANGING YOUR OPINION

18.1 If, as a result of fresh information received after you have written your report, you wish to revise your opinion, not only are you free to do so but you owe a positive duty to the court to do so and to advise the court of the reasons for your change of stance.

18.2 Experts whose minds are open and who change their opinions appropriately on the receipt of fresh information are respected by the court. Provided your original opinion was soundly based and provided there is good reason for any change of opinion, your change of stance is unlikely to be criticised by the court, although you may have to defend it in cross-examination.

18.3 It is therefore extremely important that your original opinion should be soundly based and cogently argued. It is always worth bearing in mind that although your report is written for the court and for the child, your views inevitably have a considerable impact on the lay parties to the proceedings. Particularly in disputed cases where the allegation is non-accidental injury, an unsound or untenable position taken by an expert one way or the other which then has to be revised may well be difficult for a lay party to accept. This is particularly the case where the original opinion appears to exclude abuse or exonerates an alleged participant.

18.4 You may change your opinion as a consequence of a meeting with your colleagues of the type described in Chapter 13. You should, of course, approach a meeting of experts with your mind open to the arguments of your colleagues and to the discussion which takes place. If you find those arguments properly persuasive and as a consequence change your opinion for good reason, you will need to ensure that the reasons for your change of stance are properly minuted, but, for the reasons already given, you are unlikely to be subject to any criticism from the court.

18.5 It is, however, equally important that any reasons for a change of stance are transparent. It should go without saying that you should not be bullied or coerced by your colleagues into a change of stance for reasons of convenience or any other inappropriate or improper motive. As has already been said, the courts value your independence and integrity. Any attempt, from whatever source, to tamper with that integrity is to be deprecated.

SUMMARY

18.6   Experts who change their opinions for good reason on the receipt of fresh information are respected by the court rather than criticised. However, if you change your opinion, you should always explain why you have done so.

Chapter 19

PREPARING FOR COURT

LOGISTICS

19.1   Where the medical evidence is unanimous on the point or points which the experts have been asked to address, the presence of any of the medical witnesses to give oral evidence is unlikely to be justified. If you are asked to attend court in these circumstances, you should query with the commissioning solicitor why you are being asked to attend and, in particular, whether your attendance is being required by the judge. If you take the view that you have been called to court to give evidence unnecessarily, this is an issue you should raise with the judge hearing the case, the Designated Family Judge for the particular care centre where you have been called to give evidence (see Appendix 3), the Family Division Liaison Judge for the circuit involved (see Appendix 4) or the Family Justice Council. Whilst the latter will be unable to consider individual complaints, it will be able to address issues. Doctors attending court unnecessarily and in breach of good practice by lawyers is, plainly, an issue which should be addressed.

19.2   In the past, the legal profession often treated the convenience of expert witnesses with a casualness which was both unconducive to any concept of mutual co-operation and likely to reinforce the reluctance which many of you have about giving evidence in court.

19.3   Good practice now requires lawyers to recognise that expert witnesses are busy people with many professional calls upon their time and that giving evidence in court is both time-consuming and takes them away from their clinical duties and other important professional commitments.[1]

19.4   A number of recent decisions by judges have designed to consult the convenience of expert witnesses and to try to ensure that their time is not wasted. Good practice now requires the lawyers in the case to ensure that:

(1)   a date and time for your evidence is fixed substantially in advance of the hearing, so that you can fit it into your other professional commitments;

(2)   if your oral evidence is not required, you are notified as far in advance of the hearing as possible so that you do not find yourself travelling to court only to find that you are not, after all, needed;

(3) the judge is given a sensible estimate of how long you are likely to be in the witness-box so that your evidence can be timetabled and you can fix other professional commitments around it. In particular, every effort should be made to ensure that your evidence does not exceed the time allotted for it so that you do not have to come back on another day to finish it.

19.5   Where you have been asked to attend court at a particular time on a particular day, judges hearing cases under the Children Act will normally interpose your evidence at that point, even if that means interrupting another witness. Alternatively, expert evidence in a contested case may be arranged so that experts from similar disciplines can listen to each other's evidence.

19.6   You need to be proactive in ensuring that suitable arrangements have been made for your evidence. Whilst the onus is on the lawyers to deliver proper case management, it would be sensible if your secretary or somebody on your behalf remains in regular touch with the solicitor who has commissioned your report to ensure in particular that:

(1) the case is being heard on the dates fixed for it;
(2) your evidence is still needed;
(3) a firm date and time has been set aside for your evidence;
(4) you are up to date with any recent developments in the case;
(5) there are no additional documents which have come to light since you wrote your report and which you have not seen;[2]
(6) all the relevant documents referred to in your report are before the court.

SUMMARY

19.7   The lawyers and the court should ensure that your oral evidence is fixed for a date and time which is convenient for you and that it does not exceed the time set aside. You need to play your part in ensuring that you attend court only if it is strictly necessary for you to do so.

NOTES

[1]   See in particular paragraphs 6.1 and 6.2 of Appendix C of the Protocol set out in Chapter 26.

[2]   See *Re G, S and M (Wasted Costs)* [2000] 1 FLR 52, in which I ordered a member of the bar to pay the costs incurred in requiring an expert witness to return on another occasion after she had been shown documents for the first time when giving evidence and required time to read and consider them.

Chapter 20

WITNESS SUMMONSES
(FORMERLY KNOWN AS SUBPOENAS)

20.1 Following the introduction of the Civil Procedure Rules 1998 the term 'subpoena' has been replaced for all purposes by the term 'witness summons'. A witness summons is an order to attend the court on a given date to give evidence under pain of being in contempt of court and liable to be punished if you do not attend. It is a document which has to be obtained from the court by one of the parties and it is served personally on you.

20.2 Nothing is more counter-productive to good relations between expert witnesses and lawyers than for the expert witness to be served with a witness summons, particularly if no notice of an intention to issue such a summons has been given to you. This is particularly the case if the summons requires you to attend court at very short notice or on a given day and 'each following day of the hearing until the court tells you that you are no longer required'.

20.3 If a case is properly managed, it should only be necessary to have an expert witness attend court pursuant to a witness summons in one of three circumstances where:

(1) that witness personally requests a witness summons to be issued;
(2) there is evidence that the witness has not co-operated in making arrangements to come to court to give evidence; or
(3) the interests of the child require the attendance of the witness as a matter of urgency and in circumstances which the court determines are sufficient to override other professional commitments which the witness may have.

20.4 There are certain professionals, such as health visitors and some therapists, who require to be ordered to attend court and give evidence under the compulsion of a witness summons so that they can avoid giving the impression that they are willing parties to what they or their clients may perceive as a breach of a confidential relationship. Sometimes, a professional witness may ask to be served with a witness summons as a protection against criticism for failing to be in two places at the same time.

20.5 Where it is suggested that the witness has not co-operated, the issue of a witness summons should none the less be regarded as a matter of last resort and evidence should be available to the court of non-cooperation before a witness summons is issued.[1]

20.6   If you are served with a witness summons without warning or prior consultation, you should immediately seek an explanation from the solicitor who commissioned your report or who applied for the summons. If there is a reasonable explanation for the summons and your evidence is required, it should be possible for you to negotiate a date and time at which you can attend court.

20.7   If the summons requires you to attend the court the next morning and is served out of hours, or if it is served in other circumstances which make it impossible for you to make immediate contact with the solicitor who commissioned your report, you should obey the summons if you possibly can and complain to the judge either in person or later in writing about the way you have been treated. If you cannot attend court in obedience to the summons, you should ensure that your secretary or somebody on your behalf communicates immediately with the court to explain why you cannot attend. It should then be possible for you to agree a time to attend if your evidence is really necessary. A properly organised case should, however, never reach this stage.

SUMMARY

20.8   If the system has operated properly, a witness summons should be necessary only if you require one to be issued for any reason. You do, however, need to ensure that you remain in contact with the lawyers who are making arrangements for your attendance at court in order to avoid any misunderstandings. If you are served with a summons inappropriately and you cannot negotiate a time to attend court, you should obey the summons if you possibly can and should protest. If you cannot obey it, ensure that you communicate with the court to explain why.

NOTES

1   As an indication of the reluctance of the judiciary to issue such a summons, see *Oldham MBC v GW and others* [2007] EWHC 136 (Fam) in which Ryder J said the following at paragraphs 61 and 62. (The case itself is discussed in Chapter 32.) I have called the doctors X and Y, although they are identified in the report. For a discussion on the question of whether experts should be named, see Chapter 35.

> 61.   The matter came before the High Court for re-hearing on 1 November 2005. In the light of the age of K (the child concerned) and the effect upon all concerned, time was found in the first available list on the Northern Circuit by triple listing all High Court sittings. As is often the case with urgent children matters, making scarce court time available for an essential hearing brings with it significant difficulties in getting witnesses

to attend court. Dr X repeatedly made himself available at short notice to give evidence so that the pre-existing court and clinical commitments of Dr Y could be honoured. Only after very significant efforts by the court and the lawyers involved was it possible to hear the evidence of both witnesses in chief, where they maintained the strength of their opinions. Due to the unavailability of Dr Y the cross examination of neither witness was completed.

62. Although I accept that Dr Y's commitments were very significant in that his urgent clinical duties which included reviewing the work of others had already been interrupted by another court's demands, I have never before had to threaten a witness summons against an eminent practitioner simply to ensure that the evidence in an urgent case could be heard. This court does not stand on ceremony but the heightened emotions thereby created did nothing to instil in the innocent parents any confidence that they would ever see justice done. Dr Y has apologised for the impression that was created which I readily accept was not his intention but was the accumulated pressure of high profile clinical and forensic work and a lack of court space in any location convenient to the witnesses.

Chapter 21

WHAT HAPPENS AT AND IN COURT: INTRODUCTION

21.1 Many expert witnesses find the courtroom a hostile environment. One distinguished and very experienced doctor, whom I will not name, told me in terms that 'doctors see courts in a very negative way'. This ought not to be the case in family proceedings relating to children.

21.2 Cross-examination, in particular, is perceived by some experts as a gladiatorial combat in which the lawyers make the rules and change them as they go along. This is a misconception.

21.3 I repeat one of the key messages of this Handbook. You are giving evidence to assist the judge reach a difficult decision about the welfare of a child. As His Honour Judge Harold Wilson put it in one of the cases:

> 'The game of adversarial litigation has no point when one is trying to deal with fragile and vulnerable people like small children.'[1]

21.4 Proceedings relating to children are highly emotive for the parties engaged in them. As a consequence, they need to be conducted in court in as calm and studied an atmosphere as possible. All the witnesses should be treated with courtesy by the judge and the lawyers. It is the task of both the judge and the lawyers to create and to maintain the appropriate atmosphere for calm and rational investigation of the issues.

21.5 It is the task of the judge to ensure fair play and to prevent irrelevant or hostile cross-examination. Cross-examination should go to issues, not personalities. All witnesses are entitled to be treated fairly and with courtesy, even, perhaps particularly, when their views are being rigorously tested.[2]

21.6 Whatever the reason you have been summoned to court, you should be told in advance by the solicitor who has commissioned your report why you are being asked to attend and given the issues in the case which you will be specifically asked to address in your oral evidence. If you are not given this information in good time, make sure that you ask for it before you come to court. Any last minute queries can be resolved in a short conference at court with the lawyer calling you to give evidence.

SUMMARY

21.7   The courtroom is not your normal workplace and you may feel nervous or uneasy about attending court and giving evidence. Both the lawyers and, in particular, the judge should, however, ensure that you are fairly and courteously treated and that the proceedings are conducted in a calm and rational atmosphere.

NOTES

1   *Oxfordshire County Council v M and Another* [1994] Fam 151 at 158.
2   The judicial role in holding the ring in care proceedings is critical. In criminal cases, where the function of the judge is to see that the rules of evidence are obeyed and that the case is fairly summed up to the jury, the judge is unlikely to be interventionist for fear of a perception of bias in the minds of the jury. In a family case, however, the judge should have no such inhibitions. Judges hearing family case should, accordingly, intervene if they think the lawyers are behaving inappropriately. There is no excuse for discourtesy on the part of anybody in a family case. Judges hearing care cases receive special training before they are allowed to do so. If your experience does not coincide with the principles set out in this chapter and elsewhere in this Handbook, you must make your voice heard. There are now several channels which enable you to do so: see Chapter 24 and the cross-references in that chapter.

Chapter 22

AT COURT: WHO CAN YOU TALK TO?

22.1   You arrive at court. You should have been told the name of the judge and the number of the court before you arrive. Are there any rules about who you can talk to before you actually give your evidence?

22.2   Expert witnesses are often unsure about whether or not it is proper for them to talk to counsel or solicitors or any of the parties outside the doors of the court and immediately prior to giving oral evidence. The following suggestions are offered as guidance. Ultimately, it must be a matter for you and the exercise of your professional judgment.

22.3   If it has been necessary for you to come to court, the likelihood is that this is because your report remains in contention with one or more of the parties and your oral evidence is required for that reason. It follows that, if there are to be further discussions about your evidence outside court, there must be a good reason for any such discussions.

22.4   Your report will usually have been commissioned by one of the parties. It is, therefore, perfectly proper for you to have a conference with the lawyers representing the party who commissioned your report before you go into court. The purpose of such a conference will be to ensure that you are up to date with developments both in and out of court, to ensure that you have seen all relevant documents and for the lawyer who is calling you to give evidence to discuss with you what issues will be addressed during the first part of the questioning, your examination-in-chief, which is to be conducted by that lawyer.

22.5   When you have been instructed by one party only, you should not talk to the lawyers for any of the other parties about the case without either obtaining the agreement of the lawyers for the party who commissioned your report or, at the very least, telling them that this is what you propose to do. There must, moreover, be a good reason for any such discussions. Bear in mind that the lawyer to whom you are then talking will shortly be cross-examining you in court and may wish to make use of any discrepancy between what you have said outside and what you say in the witness box.

22.6   Remember also that you are there to give evidence to the judge, not to discuss the case with the lawyers.

22.7   Where you have been instructed by the parties jointly the safest course is to adopt the same approach. Thus, it would be perfectly proper for you to have a short conference with the lawyers for the lead party (usually the lawyers instructed by the children's guardian) before giving evidence but it would be prudent to talk to any of the other parties' lawyers about the case only if there is a particular reason to do so and with the agreement of the lawyers for the lead party.

22.8   In some cases, the commissioning party may abandon reliance on the expert he has instructed. This usually occurs when you produce a report which is unhelpful to the case of the commissioning party. In such a case, if you are required to attend court, you may be called by one of the other parties or you may be called by the judge, to enable each of the parties to cross-examine you. If this occurs, you should be informed in advance either by the solicitor who commissioned the report or by the solicitor instructed by the children's guardian.

22.9   It is generally undesirable for you to have any conversation with any of the lay parties to the proceedings at court prior to giving evidence unless there is a good reason to do so and there is general agreement that you should talk to the party in question.

22.10   If you feel in difficulty about whom you should or should not talk to about the case immediately before giving evidence, the best course is to speak only to the lawyers who are going to call you to give evidence.

22.11   Nothing, however, should prevent you exchanging the normal courtesies with the parties and their lawyers outside the court. If you have not met the parents before, you may wish to be introduced to them. If you think it would be helpful to speak to them, or to their lawyers, about the case – perhaps to explain your conclusions to them – there is no reason why you should not do so if they are willing to talk to you and their lawyers agree.

22.12   In a nutshell, however, if the system is operating properly you should arrive at court in time to be brought up to date by the lawyers who commissioned your report. You should then go at once into the witness box.

SUMMARY

22.13   When arriving at court it is perfectly in order for you to have a short conference with the lawyers for the party who commissioned your report and who are calling you to give your evidence-in-chief. You should discuss the case with the other lawyers or any of the parties only if there is a particular reason to do so and if all the lawyers in the case agree that it is appropriate for you to do so. There is nothing to prevent the usual courtesies being exchanged outside the door of the court.

Chapter 23

GIVING EVIDENCE

23.1   This chapter is divided into the following sections:

(1) Addressing the judge
(2) Taking the oath or affirming
(3) Evidence-in-chief
(4) Identifying the lawyers
(5) Cross-examination
(6) Re-examination
(7) Where your evidence spans an adjournment or there is a break while you are giving evidence
(8) Questions from the judge.

23.2   Your evidence will be divided into three parts:

(1) Examination-in-chief
(2) Cross-examination
(3) Re-examination.

This chapter deals with each in turn. It begins, however, with a point of general importance which is often not fully appreciated by witnesses.

ADDRESSING THE JUDGE

23.3   Witnesses give evidence to the judge or magistrates, not to the barrister or solicitor (or, increasingly, the unrepresented litigant) asking the questions. It is, therefore, both correct and courteous to address the judge when giving evidence. High Court Judges are called either 'My Lady' or 'My Lord' according to gender: Circuit Judges, Recorders and Assistant Recorders are called 'Your Honour'. The Chair of a Lay Bench is addressed either as 'Sir' or 'Madam' according to gender. If in doubt about how to address the tribunal, ask the lawyer calling you to give your evidence-in-chief before you go into the witness box.[1]

23.4   Addressing your answers to the judge or magistrates is not only courteous and correct; it has two further advantages. First, it enables you to develop a rapport with the judge and thus prevents you from becoming engaged in a lawyer-led discussion in which the lawyer asking the questions invariably dictates their substance and the pace at which they are asked. Secondly, it gives you fractionally more time to think about what you are saying.

23.5   Most courtrooms are so designed that in order to look at the cross-examiner, the witness has to turn away from the judge. Although it is difficult, you should always try to turn back to face the judge when giving your answer. This process emphasises that you are giving evidence to the judge, not conducting a private discussion with the lawyer asking the questions.

23.6   You should always bring your notes and any relevant files with you. Alternatively, you should check in advance that the court has all the relevant material before it. Nothing irritates the court more than witnesses who do not have with them vital pieces of information contained in a file which is not in court. Your report of what was said by a person whom you have interviewed may well be challenged. You are likely to have made a contemporaneous note of your interview with the person. You may be asked if you made a note and, if so, what it said. If you do not have your notes with you, you immediately create a poor impression and your professionalism is devalued.

TAKING THE OATH OR AFFIRMING

23.7   When you go into the witness-box, you will be asked by the court usher whether you wish to take the oath or whether you wish to affirm. The oath is a promise, on the Bible or other religious text, to tell the truth. Affirmation is a promise to do so. You will be asked to read the relevant words from a printed card the usher will give you or, possibly, to repeat the words after the usher.

23.8   An affirmation carries identical weight to the oath and you have an absolute right to affirm if, for example you wish to because you have no religious beliefs. If you wish to avoid any mix-up or hesitation, either tell the usher before you go into court how you wish to take the oath or get one of the lawyers to do so.

EXAMINATION-IN-CHIEF

23.9   Examination-in-chief is the first part of your evidence and is conducted by the lawyer for the party who commissioned your report. You will be asked to identify yourself and to give your professional address and qualifications. You will then be asked to identify your report, which you will probably have loose but which will also be in a bundle of documents being used by the court, a copy of which should be in the witness-box.

23.10   Technically, the lawyer calling you should not ask you any leading questions unless they are uncontroversial. A leading question is one which either suggests a particular answer or contains the answer within the question. You may, however, sometimes hear one of the lawyers telling the lawyer conducting your examination-in-chief not to 'lead' on a controversial point or the judge might intervene in the same way.

23.11 The judge will have read your report in advance of your appearance in court. There is therefore no need for you to repeat the contents of your report in your oral evidence. The purpose of your examination-in-chief is to clarify any part of your report which the lawyer calling you may not think is clear and to invite you to comment on developments since your report was written. This may include evidence which has been given in court before you were called to give evidence.

23.12 All these matters should have been discussed with you outside court and you should not be taken by surprise. Proceedings under the Children Act 1989 are currently heard 'in chambers', that is to say in private, and unless you have asked or been asked to sit in on other evidence, you are unlikely to have heard any of the other witnesses in the case. However, if you and a colleague are both giving evidence on the same point one after the other, you may be invited to remain in court for each other's evidence.

23.13 Except in the most complex cases, your evidence-in-chief is likely to be short. In essence, your report is your evidence in chief. You will only need to give additional evidence in chief on developments in the case not covered in your report. You will then be cross-examined by each of the other lawyers in the case.

23.14 If your report has been disavowed by the party who commissioned it, or if you are jointly instructed and all the lawyers want to cross-examine you, the procedure will be slightly different. In such a case, and after you have taken the oath or affirmed, the judge is likely to ask you to identify yourself and your report and to ask you if there is anything you wish to add to your report before you are cross-examined. Then the judge may himself ask you some preliminary questions, although judicial questions normally arise both as you give your evidence and at the end when the lawyers for the parties have finished. Do not be phased by judicial interventions. They are (usually) helpful.

IDENTIFY THE LAWYERS

23.15 Particularly in care proceedings, where there are usually several parties, you may feel at a disadvantage when you go into court if you do not know the name of the lawyer asking you questions or the perspective from which the questions are coming.

23.16 If you do feel this way, you should ask the lawyer who is calling you to give evidence in chief (whose name you will know or ought to have been told) to identify for you the lawyers acting for the other parties. This can either be done before you go into court or when you are in the witness-box. You will then be able to refer to them by name in court if you wish to, and will know the perspective from which the questions they are asking you originate. Good lawyers will often volunteer this information before they begin to ask you questions.

CROSS-EXAMINATION

23.17   There are many misapprehensions and much mythology surrounding cross-examination. Its purpose, with lay witnesses, is to test their honesty and reliability – what lawyers call 'witness credibility'. With expert witnesses, its purpose is to test the validity of the opinions you have expressed. The lawyer's task is to put the client's case to you. This will, of course, include challenges to your conclusions and will, in complex medical cases, involve a close discussion of your view compared with those of your colleagues. You must therefore expect a rigorous examination of your conclusions and of your methodology. Cross-examination, if well conducted, is helpful to the judge and, if your report is well written, your conclusions sound and your methodology appropriate, you have nothing to fear. It is idle to pretend that cross-examination is a pleasurable process but you may find intelligent questions stimulating and sometimes even helpful.

23.18   Cross-examination should always be courteous. In criminal cases, where there is a jury present, judges tend to be less interventionist for fear of giving the appearance of bias. Family proceedings are quasi-inquisitorial in nature and the judge should intervene if the cross-examination becomes personal or offensive. The judge may also intervene as your evidence progresses, either to ask a question of his own or to clarify a question or answer.

23.19   As has already been explained in Chapter 4, in family proceedings the court's enquiry into the welfare of the child is 'non-adversarial'. This does not, of course, mean that contentious issues of fact and opinion do not arise in proceedings relating to children and will not arise during your evidence. If you have expressed firm opinions, you must expect to be firmly challenged on them.

23.20   However, cross-examination, particularly of an expert witness, should always go to issues, not personalities and your credibility as an expert should only ever be in issue if you have stepped outside the bounds of your expertise, gone inappropriately beyond your instructions or adopted a methodology for the preparation of your report which is open to criticism.[2] Even then, the cross-examination should be directed to the validity of your conclusions and the consequences of any error you may have made for the children concerned in the case.

23.21 If you are anxious about cross-examination, remember that you will almost always know more about your subject that the lawyer asking the questions or the judge listening to you. On the other hand, the lawyer knows what the next question will be.

FOUR GOLDEN RULES

23.22 There are four golden rules.

(1) Always answer the question put to you. That sounds easy but it is not. Do not seek to evade the question or answer what you think will be the next question. If you cannot answer the question, perhaps because it takes you outside the ambit of your expertise, say so. This is very important. Do not be drawn into areas outside your expertise. Alternatively, seeks the judge's advice if you think you should not be discussing a particular topic because it is not in your field.
(2) Take your time. Do not allow the questioner to rush you. Do not hesitate to ask for time to think if you are asked a particularly difficult question. The judge wants your carefully considered opinion.
(3) Try to keep your answers short and to the point. The judge wants answers, not a lecture.
(4) Never try to score points or get into an argument with the questioner. Doing so is inconsistent with your role as an expert witness and is unlikely to help the judge. The judge wants your objective professional opinion. It is for the lawyers to argue the case.

23.23 If you are asked to give a 'yes or no' answer to a question which you feel requires qualification, either say: 'the answer to your question is "yes" (or "no" as the case may be) but that needs to be qualified by …' (you can then provide the qualification). Alternatively, if the question simply cannot be answered 'yes' or 'no', say so. 'I am very sorry, My Lord/Lady/Your Honour, but I simply cannot give a yes or no answer to that question. It all depends on …' (then explain your reasons).

23.24 Since the judge's objective will be to keep the atmosphere in court calm and rational, try not to become exasperated if the lawyer's questioning demonstrates a fundamental ignorance of the topic under discussion. Once again, the best course is to talk to the judge. The more in sorrow than in anger approach is always to be preferred: 'My Lord/Lady/Your Honour, I think the question Mr/Ms X has asked demonstrates a misunderstanding of the position …' (you can then explain the misapprehension).

23.25 If you feel the cross-examination is repetitive or offensive, once again address the judge. 'My Lord/Lady/Your Honour, I think I have already answered that question but if you wish I will go over it again'. If you think the cross-examiner is implying something offensive, say something like: 'My Lord/ Lady/Your Honour, I am not clear about the implication behind the question but if it is being suggested that I have misunderstood the nature of the child's injuries, I disagree'.

26.26   Never hesitate to make appropriate concessions to the cross-examiner. Experts who are willing to make proper concessions are always more respected by a judge than those who stick to their opinion through thick and thin.

23.27   You should always provide an opinion, not an argument. The expert who is perceived as arguing a case tends to lose objectivity and gives the impression of partiality.

23.28   Cross-examination should not be an ordeal. It is healthy for every profession to have its opinions and its methodology tested by outsiders and there is no reason why you should not find cross-examination stimulating and helpful to you in clarifying your thought process and conclusions.

23.29   Remember always, the golden rule of expert evidence is that you are in court to help the judge reach a conclusion about the child. The case is not about you and, as has already been stated, you should not be subject to any personal attack unless you have broken the rules in some specific way or fallen below the high standards of your profession.

RE-EXAMINATION

23.30   The purpose of re-examination, which is conducted by the lawyer who conducted your examination-in-chief, is to clarify points made in cross-examination. (In adversarial litigation its object is to repair the damage done in cross-examination.) For the lawyer, re-examination is difficult because the rule is that leading questions are not allowed. This is because suggesting an answer to a witness who has said something different in cross-examination rarely has any evidential value. Many lawyers do not attempt re-examination, particularly with a competent expert witness.

WHERE YOUR EVIDENCE SPANS AN ADJOURNMENT OR THERE IS A BREAK WHILE YOU ARE GIVING EVIDENCE

23.31   The normal rule is that if there is a break in the proceedings while you are in the middle of your evidence, you should not talk to anybody about the case until your evidence is concluded. The obvious reason for this is the risk that your evidence may be contaminated or influenced by something said to you outside the courtroom. If, for any reason, you want the rule relaxed, you should ask the judge before the court breaks whether it is in order for you to talk to a particular person.

23.32   For the same reasons, once your evidence is concluded, you should not talk to any of your colleagues or any of the other witnesses about the case or your evidence until their evidence is concluded. Always bear in mind that unauthorised publication of information relating to proceedings in chambers is a contempt of court.

QUESTIONS FROM THE JUDGE

23.33   The judge is quite likely to ask you questions, either during the course of your evidence or when the lawyers have concluded. Lay magistrates are far less likely to do so and their questions will usually come through the chair.

SUMMARY

23.34   Your evidence will consist of taking the oath, examination-in-chief, cross-examination and, possibly, re-examination. You may take the oath or affirm. It is courteous, as well as likely to help put you at your ease, if the lawyers or the various parties identify themselves. This can either be done in court or you can ask the lawyer who is calling you to give evidence to identify the other lawyers in the case. Do not talk to anyone about the case during breaks in your evidence or until the case is over.

You have come to court to give evidence to the judge. Talk to the judge, not to the lawyer asking you questions. And always bring your file.

So far as cross-examination is concerned, remember that you are the expert and that everybody in court knows less about the subject matter of your evidence than you do, apart from your fellow experts. Answer the question. Do not lose your temper. If you want time to think, ask for it. Do not engage in an argument with the lawyer cross-examining you. Make concessions where appropriate. Give the court your opinion, not an argument in favour of one side rather than the other.

NOTES

1   Appendix 5 contains a guide to judicial titles.
2   See Chapter 1. For another recent example, see *Re L (Children)* [2006] EWCA Civ 1282.

Chapter 24

FEEDBACK AND COMPLAINTS

24.1 You are entitled to feedback after the case is over and, if it is not provided, you should not hesitate to ask for it. Paragraph 7.1 of Appendix C to the Protocol[1] places an obligation on the solicitor instructing you to provide feedback. This usually takes the form of a letter from the commissioning solicitor or, where the judgment of the court has been transcribed, a copy of the judgment. Leave to disclose the judgment to you should, however, formally be obtained from the court, although this can and should be done at the end of the hearing itself, when the judge directs a transcript of the judgment. If, on the other hand, the judge has reserved judgment and put it into writing, there is no reason why you should not receive a copy of it.

24.2 You may feel you have been badly treated in a number of ways. You may have been inadequately instructed; you may not have received all the relevant documents; the parties may not have co-operated with you; you may feel that the lawyers or the judge have been discourteous; you may have been given no notification, or only very late notification, that your evidence was no longer required; you may have been called to court unnecessarily or kept hanging about at court; the time set aside for your evidence may not have been sufficient; you may have been served at home with a witness summons. These are only examples – there may be others.

24.3 Each care centre has a Circuit Judge who is the Designated Family Judge (DFJ) for that care centre. He or she will often chair the local branch of the Family Justice Council. He or she may therefore be a suitable first port of call for matters of practice which are of particularly local concern. A list of care centres and DFJs is given in Appendix 3.

24.4 In addition, each circuit has a High Court Family Division Liaison Judge (FDLJ), one of whose functions is to ensure the smooth running of family proceedings on the circuit. Any complaint which you feel should be addressed at a higher level than the local DFJ should, therefore, in the first instance, be addressed to the FDLJ for the circuit concerned. The names of the FDLJs and identification of their circuits are set out in Appendix 4. Each is based at the Royal Courts of Justice in London, the address of which is Strand, London, WC2A 2LL. If you need to write to one of them, do so at this address.

24.5   In addition, there is now the Experts Committee of the Family Justice Council (FJC). Whilst this body has no disciplinary jurisdiction and will not be able to resolve individual complaints, it is there to address issues which arise from such complaints. If the treatment you have received thus involves an issue of practice which has application to others, you should not hesitate to make contact with it.[2]

SUMMARY

24.6   You are entitled to feedback. If you do not get it, ask for it. If you have good cause to feel you have been badly treated, you should not hesitate to say so. Inter-disciplinary co-operation in proceedings under the Children Act is a continuing process. Each discipline needs to learn from the other. Lawyers and judges expect a great deal of experts. The legal profession therefore needs to know what is acceptable to you in the way you are treated and what is not. Use the Designated Family Judges and your Family Division Liaison Judge. Also alert the Family Justice Council to issues which arise from the way you have been treated.

NOTES

1   See Chapter 26 where Appendix C to the Protocol is set out.
2   See Chapter 27 and Appendix 2 which deal with the FJC and its personnel.

Chapter 25

PAYMENT OF EXPERTS' FEES AND CHARGES

PEGGY RAY

INTRODUCTION

25.1 You will, of course, wish to be paid promptly for the work you undertake, whether you are instructed as an expert witness or because you have a direct clinical involvement with a patient involved in the proceedings. This will include being paid for time spent in reading and considering papers and documents, undertaking interviews or examinations, discussions and meetings with others (where appropriate and necessary) corresponding with solicitors, preparing and writing reports, attending at court and travelling.[1]

25.2 As you will have gathered from earlier chapters, in family proceedings it is the parties who, through their solicitors, instruct you. In legal terms, the position is that you enter into a contract to provide your services as an expert with the *solicitor*, not the party he represents; and it is the solicitor (or, more accurately, the partners in the firm of the solicitor instructing you) who is legally bound to pay the reasonable charges for your work. It is also important for you to note your basic legal relationship with the solicitor does not depend on how solicitors themselves are funded to act for their clients.[2]

25.3 One of the most frequent complaints heard from experts in family proceedings is of the problem experienced getting paid. Various attempts have been made to ease this process and messages of good practice have been sent to instructing lawyers. Some problems do continue but there are steps which you can take to minimise the potential for them. These are set out later in this chapter.

25.4 The critical issue, in relation to dealing most effectively with the question of your fees, is to understand the payment framework in which you are instructed. The mechanisms for those instructing you will be significantly different in different kinds of cases. These differences should not of themselves make any to difference to you. You are the expert; you have done the work and you are entitled to be properly paid for it. However, knowing which buttons to press to ensure speedy payment will help avoid both misunderstandings and delay.

THE TWO DIFFERENT CATEGORIES OF CASES INVOLVING CHILDREN

25.5   As was explained in Chapter 3, it is most likely that you will be instructed in public law proceedings, that is to say care proceedings involving a local authority, in which the court will be concerned with the issue of significant harm caused or likely to be caused to children by their parents. Private law proceedings are usually only between parents, although in more complex cases the child or children can be separately represented by a children's guardian as well as by a solicitor.[3] Experts are increasingly being used in the more complex private law cases.

25.6   Most public law proceedings involve being paid through the legal aid system, now known as 'public funding'. The legal aid / public funding system is administered by the Legal Services Commission (LSC). Private law proceedings, on the other hand, may be funded by the parties paying their own costs (and therefore – through their solicitors – your fees) or by the LSC. Sometimes, in private law proceedings, one side is publicly funded and the other is not. Children, where they obtain separate representation in private law proceedings, are usually publicly funded.[4]

PUBLIC LAW PROCEEDINGS

25.7   In public law proceedings, the parents of the child or children who are the subject of the proceedings are nearly always parties to the care proceedings and are automatically entitled to legal aid whatever their means. The child or children concerned are almost invariably represented at public expense by a solicitor and a guardian.[5] It follows that in most public law cases all the parties will be funded by the taxpayer in one way or another.

25.8   Since November 2003 the payment of experts in care proceedings has been regulated in these cases by the Protocol.[6]

25.9   An important feature of the Protocol is the change in the way the payment for expert evidence is managed by the court. In the past, solicitors acting for parties seeking to adduce expert evidence raised the matter before the judge, obtained permission and negotiated the rates and timescales with the expert concerned. Apart from those acting for a local authority, this often involved an application to the LSC for 'prior authority' to commission the expert at a particular rate up to a specified limit. This guaranteed payment of fees up to the limit authorised but could be a lengthy process.

25.10   Under the Protocol, the solicitor has to obtain *from* you information which includes confirmation of hourly rates and an estimate of the overall number of hours to be spent, not only in conducting any assessments / interviews and writing reports but also in attending meetings of experts or professionals and in attending court. In other words, you are being asked for an estimate of the totality of your fees for the case. This has to be done no later than five days before the Case Management Conference (CMC).[7] In practice, this is likely to be within five days of the solicitor's approach to you. Complying with this requirement is an important and often underestimated task.

25.11 Obviously, your ability to respond constructively will depend on the quality of the information provided by the commissioning solicitor. When you cannot give an exact figure, and have to provide an estimate, it must be as realistic as you can make it. You should spell out any uncertainties. However, if inadequate information is given, it is essential that you make it clear, in writing and as soon as possible, that it is impossible for you to comply with the requirements of the Protocol for this reason.

25.12 It is important to note that, since a number of cases in 2004 and 2005, it has become clear that the LSC will not fund any expenses relating to the treatment, therapy or training of parents or children.[8] This includes any interventions of a rehabilitative nature. The Funding Code (which sets out those matters which properly fall within the scope of a legal aid / public funding certificate) was amended in July 2005 to make this distinction clear. The only expert or assessment work which will be funded is that which is required as substantive evidence for the court process. This includes an assessment of a parent's capacity to change (although it is arguable whether an assessment of a parent's insight into the need to change and their ability to act on that insight consistently could be covered). These difficulties arise most frequently in relation to residential assessments under interim care orders, a subject to which this Handbook is not primarily addressed, although often experts are commissioned to report during the course of a residential assessment.[9]

25.13 The duty of the solicitor proposing to instruct you is to serve a prescribed form on the other parties to the proceedings and lodge it at court no later than two days before the CMC. The form has to include the following information in relation to you and to any other proposed expert:

(1) Who will be responsible for the instruction.
(2) Whether the instruction will be made jointly between two or more parties or is more properly obtained by only one (eg on behalf of the child).
(3) The likely cost of the report on both an hourly and global basis.
(4) The apportionment of costs of jointly instructed experts as between the Local Authority and the legally aided / publicly funded parties.

25.14 As can be seen, at this stage the Protocol expects there to be a quick exchange of comprehensive information between the solicitor and youself. Because of the commitments of both of you, it can often take four or five days to make initial telephone contact and some of the time limits set out in the Protocol have proven to be unrealistic. The courts have made it clear that the Protocol is to provide guidance rather than prescription and of necessity it may have to be modified in an individual case. However, from your point of view it is useful to have a schedule of charges readily available to be emailed or faxed to an instructing solicitor. A suggested pro forma is set out in Appendix 6.

25.15   You may be asked to accept certain limitations on the way you are paid. You may be asked, for example, to accept payment of the fees agreed 'subject to detailed assessment'. This means that if your fees are reduced by the LSC or the court at the end of the case you will be bound by that reduction. It will be a matter for you whether you are prepared to accept an instruction on these terms.

25.16   At the CMC the remit of your instruction and the estimate you have provided will be examined by the court and approval to your instruction and fees will either be confirmed or refused.

THE LETTER OF INSTRUCTION

25.17   The substantive issues to be dealt with in the letter of instruction have been addressed in Chapter 10. In relation to fees, within five days of the CMC the solicitor instructing you is expected to file at court and send you an agreed letter of instruction. The information it contains should include the funding basis on which you are instructed, including the hourly rate and overall limit authorised by the court, when you will be paid and any limits on the charges you may make. There should also be a brief explanation of the process called the 'detailed assessment' of costs in the County Court and High Court.

25.18   If the letter of instruction cannot be agreed, the court has the power to decide its contents, including, in the event of a dispute, the level of your fees.

PAYMENT

25.19   Under the Protocol, it is the court itself, rather than the LSC, which should specify your fees, both in terms of the hourly rate and the overall global limit. Once this is done, the solicitor can apply for your fees 'on account' from the LSC in the knowledge that the court has, in effect, sanctioned the payment and there should be no risk that either you or the solicitor will be faced with an overpayment when the costs are considered at the conclusion of the case. There should be no need for the solicitor to apply for a prior authority from the LSC, nor for you to insist on such an authority although, as a matter of law, only such an authority can bind the costs assessing body (whether that is the court or a regional office of the LSC).

25.20 Once your work is completed, it is important that you deliver an invoice to the solicitor instructing you as soon as possible. It should be comprehensive and, in the case of a joint instruction, it should make it clear whether the sum sought is the total from all parties or a single party's share.[10]

25.21 Keep a diary note of the terms of payment agreed in order that your invoice can be chased promptly if necessary.

COMMON PROBLEMS ENCOUNTERED BY EXPERTS IN RESPECT OF PAYMENT AND HOW TO USE THE PROTOCOL EFFECTIVELY

Joint instructions

25.22 On many occasions you will be jointly instructed, with one solicitor (usually the child's solicitor) being the lead solicitor. In the past, the responsibility for payment of fees would be split between the various parties responsible for the joint instruction. This meant that you may have had to chase three or four parties for payment of relatively small sums.

25.23 To support the Protocol, the LSC has introduced a method for solicitors to claim jointly incurred fees which hopefully will avoid this problem in future. Now, the lead solicitor can make one claim from the LSC for *all* of the contributions of the publicly funded parties, which will be paid to each party's solicitor. Please note, however, that this does *not* include the Local Authority. Each solicitor will then be in funds to make payment directly to you, or if ordered by the court, to make payment to the lead solicitor. The lead solicitor will then be in a position to make payment to you. This procedure will apply to both 'interim' and final bills. Please note also, however, that no such claims can be made without a proper invoice from you and, moreover, one which comes within the limits approved by the court.

25.24 Usually, the court will have made a direction providing (1) for specific authority to enable the lead solicitor to make such a 'unified claim' at the CMC or later and (2) allocating the responsibility for payment to you as being that of the lead solicitor. Lead solicitors may be more willing to submit to such a responsibility if they can be sure a claim is made promptly, although they will still be in a position of having to recover funds from the other parties. It may be advisable for you to confirm that such a direction should be sought when accepting an instruction.

25.25 A suggested form of such a direction is:

That the costs of [the expert] be apportioned between (A, B & C), those fees to be discharged by the lead solicitor within X days of receipt of [the expert's] invoice.

25.26   This procedure only applies to those parties who are legally aided / publicly funded. Therefore the lead solicitor (if directed to be responsible for payment) will still have the responsibility of obtaining the funds to pay your fees from – for example – the Local Authority. However, the change is that this will not be your responsibility but that of the lead solicitor. In other words, you should now be able to deal only with the lead solicitor in respect of payment.

Sole instruction

25.27   If you have been instructed by one party alone, then it is to that party's solicitor that you should look for payment. This should be straightforward. However, see below for enforcement if you have problems.

LATE PAYMENT – WITHIN AUTHORISED LIMITS

25.28   If the court has approved your instruction and if you have both reported and rendered an invoice, there is no reason (subject to the efficiency of the LSC and the competence of your instructing solicitor) why payment should not be made promptly. Again, it is important for you to understand how the solicitor receives funds. Once your invoice is received, a form can be completed and sent to the LSC requesting a payment 'on account'. Payments are made by the LSC to solicitors every two weeks or every month (depending on the size of practice) and payment should come through within eight weeks of the claim. Certainly, in London, payment is usually quicker than this but the time can vary from region to region – as it depends on the work received by the relevant LSC regional office at any given time. The payment has to be processed by the solicitor's practice but should not take more than a week or so and payment can then be made to you.

25.29   Allowing for all of these caveats, if you have not received payment within say 12 weeks of the invoice, you should write a letter to the solicitor instructing you asking if a claim has been made from the LSC. Ultimately, it is open to you to write to the judge himself raising the issue of non-payment. A solicitor should be worried if this step were to be taken and a threat to do just this might be sufficient. If not, the court, under the Protocol, can act as the expert's 'bailiff' and direct the solicitor to explain why payment has not been made or take any other action thought appropriate. You can also complain to the instructing solicitor's firm (always address any email or letter to the Senior Partner) using their complaints procedure. See below for other methods of enforcement.

LATE PAYMENT – FOR WORK OVER ANY AUTHORISED LIMITS

25.30 If you undertake work which exceeds any limit authorised by the court, the question of the payment of your fees over that limit will be subject to a process called a 'detailed assessment'. This is a process where the court (or in cases being dealt with in the Family Proceedings Court, the LSC) checks the solicitors' bill and your fees contained in it. Because of the detailed scrutiny undertaken by the court or the LSC, it is important that you keep a detailed and accurate record of all of the work you have undertaken including what work was done, how long it took and the dates on which it was undertaken. Any unexpected difficulties (for example, the late arrival of an interpreter which lengthens the interview time or the failure of an interviewee to attend an interview) should be noted. This detail can be part of your invoice or attached as a schedule of work. Any expenses incurred should also be noted.

25.31 A court assessment can take months although the LSC has performance targets for processing claims. In the case of an assessment by the court (rather than the LSC) it is only after this process has been completed that the LSC can make payment and you can be paid without risk of overpayment by your instructing solicitor.

25.32 If the court or LSC considers part of your fee unreasonable, it can disallow that part of the fee. This is rare but most commonly comes up in relation to 'cancellation charges'. If there are good reasons why you could not undertake other work in the lost time, the court usually will allow such charges (the most obvious example is where you have travelled to a failed appointment). Otherwise, the court is likely to take the view that there was other work you could have done and will not authorise an 'administrative' charge or cancellation fee. This is another reason by your invoices need to be clear and comprehensive.

25.33 Because of these difficulties, it is important that you keep a close eye on how costs are accruing as the case progresses. Once the costs get near to any authorised limit it is important that you contact the solicitor instructing you in writing informing him that more funds must be authorised to complete the work. This must be done promptly, both to enable the solicitor to obtain the necessary further authority either from the court or the LSC and to avoid a delay in your own work. Again as detailed an estimate (in writing) as possible will avoid problems later.

PRIVATE LAW CASES

25.34 In these cases, you will be instructed either by the parents' solicitors solely or jointly, or by the child's guardian (usually an officer from CAFCASS[11]) who will have instructed a solicitor. It is increasingly the case that the parents may be privately funded or acting in person and it is only the child who is in receipt of public funding.

25.35   The Protocol does not apply to private law cases. Therefore, the regime of the court approving an expert's fees does not apply and where the expert is being paid under a party's legal aid / public funding certificate, the old pre-Protocol procedure applies.

25.36   Briefly, this procedure entails solicitors obtaining an estimate of your charges. They then apply to the LSC for 'permission' or prior authority to incur these charges under their client's legal aid / public funding certificate. The LSC requires sufficient information to justify both your involvement in principle and the payment of your charges. In theory, solicitors are required to obtain competitive quotes from a number of experts. However, because of the general shortage of experts, particularly those who may be available to report within the cases' timetable, more than one quote is usually impossible. Solicitors then submit their request for authority on a prescribed form. It should not take more than two to three weeks for the form to be processed. However, in London the experience of the LSC is that often the form is lost and has to be re-submitted (on occasions more than once). It is only after this authority has been given that the solicitor will have a guarantee as to payment and only to the extent of the limit requested. If further work is commissioned, an application for permission to pay for further work will have to be made.

PRIVATELY FUNDED CASES

25.37   In privately funded cases, the solicitor who instructs you will be acting on behalf of his client who is funding the costs of the case personally. Solicitors are under a professional obligation to keep their clients informed of the costs of the case.[12] You will be asked therefore to give an estimate of your fees in advance.

25.38   As already stated, what it is important to understand is that your contract for work and payment is with the solicitor. This means that if the solicitor has failed to recover sufficient funds from the client to pay your bills (provided they fall within the agreed estimate of costs) the solicitor must nevertheless meet your invoice. It is for the solicitor to then try and recover the money from the client.

ENFORCEMENT

25.39   As already explained, there are several mechanisms for being instructed and therefore there are a number of different mechanisms available to enforce an unpaid invoice. Some of these mechanisms are case type specific, others apply to all types of cases. Dealing with case specific routes first:

(1)   Publicly funded cases (public law cases)

25.40   In public law cases, the Protocol applies. This adds an extra measure of enforcement for you if you have not been paid. Initially, it will be the court which has sanctioned your work as an expert. In theory, the court should have authorised a fee limit although in practice this rarely happens. In any event the first step to take (assuming reminder letters and calls to the solicitor instructing you have not worked) is to write to the judge who was allocated to the case. You may have given evidence and should know who this is. If not, the child's solicitor is the most likely to be able to help or the court itself. Your letter to the judge should set out the attempts you have made to recover payment and who is responsible for that payment (see above). The court should then write to the solicitor on your behalf. This may initially be simply a copy of your letter forwarded on to the solicitor.

25.41   If this does not succeed, you should write again to the court and ask for the matter to be placed before the judge with a view to having a hearing listed for the non-paying solicitor to attend. The solicitor is likely to want to avoid this if possible, as it will involve an unnecessary hearing and the professional embarrassment of attending before the court to explain the delay in payment.

(2)   Publicly funded cases (private law)

25.42   As already stated, these cases are not governed by the Protocol and therefore the court that dealt with the case will not have a role to play in relation to your fees and charges. The solicitor instructing you should have no difficulty in recovering your fees from the LSC subject to the process of detailed assessment.[13] It is likely that the solicitor will have recovered your fees and will have overlooked accounting to you. There may be complex accounting queries on his file. Occasionally, the solicitor will have neglected to claim your fees from the LSC. This is not your responsibility and should not impact on your entitlement to be paid. If reminder letters and telephone calls have not been successful, try writing to the senior partner of the firm concerned asking for confirmation of the following:

- Has the solicitor's bill been submitted to the LSC?
- Did the claim include your fees in full?

- Has the solicitor been paid and if so, when?
- What are the proposals to pay you?

25.43   Also in the letter you should threaten to take the matter further (see paragraph **25.50**) if you are not paid within a set period of time (say 7 to 14 days). Keep copies of all letters to the solicitor and put the period you have set for a reply in your diary.

25.44   You could try writing to the LSC direct but this is not likely to be successful. You would need to have the legal aid certificate numbers of the client or children involved for the LSC to trace the claim. The LSC may, however, be able to confirm if a final bill has been submitted and paid.

(3)   Privately funded cases

25.45   As already stated, the contract for your work in these cases is between you and the solicitor instructing you. This means that to enforce payment you are in the same position as any contractor trying to recover a civil debt.

(4)   General steps of enforcement

25.46   The steps to be taken are set out below as they are common to other kinds of cases in which the steps set out above have not succeeded.

(5)   Complaints

25.47   All solicitors are required to have complaints procedure, details of which you should receive on request. Most require a complaint to be formally made in writing. A nominated person within the firm should then deal with your complaint within a specified period. If the question of payment cannot be satisfactorily dealt with in this way, the nominated complaints partner should inform you of how you can take the matter further.

25.48   An alternative course is to complain either to the Children Panel or to the Solicitors Regulation Authority. Many solicitors who undertake children's work are members of the Children Panel. This is a panel of solicitors who specialise in children cases. In order to be on the Panel they have to undergo a rigorous examination. Membership is for a period of five years, after which the solicitor has to undergo re-accreditation if he wishes to remain on the panel. Membership of the Panel entitles the solicitor to an enhanced rate of payment by the LSC and therefore loss of membership (or a complaint which may jeopardise re-accreditation) can have serious financial consequences.

25.49   If your instructing solicitor is a member of the Children Panel, that fact will appear on the firm's headed notepaper. Your letter of complaint should then be addressed to the Administrator of the Children Panel at the Solicitors Regulation Authority, Ipsley Court, Berrington Close, Redditch, Worcestershire

B98 0TD, www.sra.org.uk. The official there should contact the Panel member on your behalf.

25.50   Alternatively all solicitors are accountable to The Legal Complaints Service, part of but independent of the Law Society. A letter of complaint can be sent to the office at Victoria Court, 8 Dormer Place, Leamington Spa, Warwickshire CV32 5AE (www.legalcomplaints.org.uk). The office may take the view that a simple case of non-payment of fees is not a matter for them on the grounds that they are concerned only with professional misconduct. However, it is can be argued that non-payment of fees for services relating to a client's affairs is not behaviour expected of a solicitor and therefore amounts to professional misconduct.

25.51   In all cases, if these preliminary efforts have not been effective in recovering your fees you should consider the option of pursuing the matter through the courts as a civil debt (legally a breach of your contract with the solicitor to pay you). This will include cases in which the limit endorsed by the Protocol has been exceeded or, after detailed assessment, the court has not authorised the level of fees charged.

25.52   Clearly you will have to make a commercial decision about whether to proceed, particularly in those cases where the court has made a detailed assessment and has not allowed them in full. If you wish to proceed, you will need to write a formal letter before action to the Senior Partner of the firm of solicitors instructing you. This should set out the details of the invoice(s) which remain unpaid and clearly state that unless payment is received within 7 or 14 days you will be issuing proceedings against the firm for the recovery of the fees. It might be helpful to send the letter recorded delivery. Keep a copy.

25.53   If that does not elicit a response, you can then consider issuing proceedings in the County Court for the recovery of the fees. This is simpler than it seems and in an increasing number of courts can be undertaken online. It does not have to be in the court local to you or the solicitor, although if the claim is contested the solicitor will have the opportunity to have the case transferred to their local court. It is likely that at this point your invoice will be met if your invoices and information are accurate and clear.

SOME PRACTICAL SUGGESTIONS

25.54   Set up a standard document which can be emailed or faxed, setting out your scale of charges – specify in that document the hourly costs of travel, interviewing or attending meetings, report writing and attending court (usually expressed as half or whole days).[14] Ensure the rates you are charging are within the scale of charges made by others undertaking similar work.

25.55 Demand sufficient information from the solicitor who makes the initial approach for you to get a pretty accurate picture of what you are being asked to do – how much reading, how many people to see / interview, at home or elsewhere, how many meetings are likely (are other experts involved?) etc. A standard letter should be set up which can be modified as necessary asking that this information is provided. In an urgent case this information may need to be obtained / given by telephone.

25.56 When giving an estimate, make it clear that it may have to be revised and ensure that it is revised promptly in light of any change in circumstances or instruction. Ensure that any revised estimate is agreed before proceeding.

25.57 Keep clear, comprehensive and accurate records of the time spent on a case as it progresses.

25.58 Keep copies of all correspondence received and sent in relation to fees.

25.59 Set up a pro forma invoice with details of time spent for each activity either as a separate schedule or as part of the invoice.[15]

25.60 Keep a good diary system to ensure reminders for payment are chased promptly.

FUTURE PROPOSALS / CHANGES

25.61 There are a number of proposals for change which are likely to have either a direct or indirect impact on the payment of your fees in Children Act cases.

FIXED FEES

25.62 From October 2007 it is extremely likely that all solicitors undertaking publicly funded children cases will be subject to a regime of fixed fees. This means that they will be paid a fixed fee for each case. However, it has now been decided that disbursements (such as your fees) will not be included in that fixed fee but payable in addition to it. The fee limit is low and, as an expert, you may experience less attention in terms of correspondence and contact than previously was the case. The instructing solicitor will keep you updated with documents but will be anxious not to undertake any more work than is absolutely necessary and you may find your day-to-day dealings are with a junior member of staff.

25.63 You are entitled to be paid regardless of whether the solicitor will lose money on the case but it can be anticipated that there will be tighter agreements made as to financial limits and you will need to be more careful that any work over and above any agreed limit is expressly authorised and confirmed in writing.

THE REVIEW OF THE PROTOCOL

25.64 As mentioned in Chapter 26, the Protocol is in the process of being revised. It is currently unclear whether the revisions will impact on the payment of experts' fees.

THE CHIEF MEDICAL OFFICER'S REPORT OCTOBER 2006

25.65 The Chief Medical Officer undertook a comprehensive investigation into the role played by medical experts in cases involving safeguarding children (*Bearing Good Witness*) published in October 2006. Although his proposals, if implemented, would have a radical effect on the manner in which expert evidence is obtained and funded, it is unlikely – even if his recommendations are accepted by government – that they would be implemented during the lifetime of this Handbook. They are not, accordingly, set out in this chapter.

LSC CONSULTATIONS

(1) The Funding Code

25.66 A consultation has just concluded on the scope of the Funding Code in relation to residential assessments (see paragraph **25.12**). It has been proposed that residential assessments including viability assessments (and specifically the assessment of a parents' capacity to change and / or the assessment of a family for the purposes of rehabilitation) will be excluded. It is proposed that any work undertaken by way of residential assessment will have to be funded by a local authority without contribution from the legally aided / publicly funded parties. The outcome of this consultation is not yet known.

(2) Experts Fees

25.67 The LSC will shortly be undertaking a consultation on the question of the payment of experts' fees in Children Act cases. This is likely to propose the payment of your fees at prescribed rates which will be fixed by the LSC. Solicitors are currently paid on the basis of fixed fees based on prescribed rates for their legal work and it is suggested that you too will be limited in terms of your fees in this way. There is likely to be a proposed fee based on work undertaken for preparation, interviewing and writing your report. It is also likely there will be a separate fee payable for attending court and for travel or waiting. It is not known when these changes will be implemented but it is likely to be within 12 months.

25.68   Experts undertaking work within the criminal courts are already subject to prescribed rates.

SUMMARY

25.69   Although this chapter contains a great deal of detail and may seem somewhat off-putting, it has had to examine what happens if things go wrong. Most solicitors engaged in children work – and particularly those who are on the Children Panel – are hardworking, committed and enthusiastic. It is not in their interests to antagonise you by dragging their feet in the process of making sure you are paid. They will probably want to use your services in another case and will not want to be refused on the grounds that you have had a bad experience over payment.

NOTES

[1]   See the model fee note at Appendix 7.

[2]   Thus in *Re A (Family Proceedings: Expert Witness)* [2002] 1 FLR 723, a solicitor who had not obtained the court's permission to instruct the expert was personally liable for his fees: see Chapter 31.

[3]   The separate representation of children in private law proceedings is currently the subject of active debate, in which, of course, the question of resources looms large. This need not concern you but you should be aware of it.

[4]   This is because the judge will have ordered separate representation and so the child will pass the LSC's merits test. Children are also very unlikely to have any means of their own and so can usually pass the LSC's means tests. All attempts by the LSC to alter the means test by amalgamating parental resources with those of their children have been firmly resisted by the legal profession.

[5]   Section 41(1) of the Children Act 1989 requires the court to appoint a guardian for a child who is the subject of care proceedings 'unless satisfied that it is not necessary to do so in order to safeguard his interests'. In practice, a guardian is invariably appointed and the guardian then appoints a solicitor to represent the child. Unless one has already been appointed by the court: – see Family Proceedings Rules 1991, 4.11A(1)(a). Separate representation of children is automatic in public law proceedings for the obvious reason that the consequences for the child following local authority intervention can be momentous. The dual system of representation by guardian and solicitor has become known as the 'tandem' model and is designed to ensure that the interests of the child or children concerned are fully protected.

[6]   Appendix C to the Protocol sets out the procedure which should be followed when an expert is instructed: see Chapter 26 where Appendix C is set out. In relation to the provision of information about your likely fees, see in particular, paragraph 2.2 of the Protocol and paragraph **25.10** where the effect of paragraph 2.2 is set out.

7   Under Step 4 of the Protocol, in its current form, the target time for the Case Management Conference (CMC) is between 15 and 60 days from the date on which the proceedings were instituted. The objective of the CMA is to consider what case management directions are necessary (1) to ensure that a fair hearing of the proceedings takes place: and (2) to timetable the proceedings so that the final hearing is completed within or before the recommended hearing winder. See also paragraph **26.4**.

8   *Kent County Council v G* [2005] UKHL 68.

9   The leading cases on the subject of residential assessments, carried out under interim care orders made pursuant to section 38(6) of the Children Act 1989 are the two decisions of the House of Lords. *Re C (A Minor) (Interim Care Order: Residential Assessment)* [1997] AC 489 and *Re G (A Minor) (Interim Care Order: Residential Assessment)* [2005] UKHL 68, [2006] 1 AC 576 and the more recent decision of the Court of Appeal in *Re L and H (Residential Assessments)* [2007] EWCA Civ 213.

10   For a model fee note, see Appendix 7.

11   The Children and Families Court Advisory Support Service – see the note in Appendix 10.

12   Solicitors Code of Conduct 2007, r 2.03.

13   'Detailed assessment' is, in essence, the process whereby a costs judge assesses the amount of costs (including experts' fees) reasonably payable. Usually this is undertaken to ascertain how much one party should pay another but a detailed assessment of a publicly funded litigant's costs determines the LSC's liability for that litigant's costs.

14   A suggested pro forma for such a document is set out in Appendix 6.

15   A suggested pro forma for such a document is set out in Appendix 7.

Chapter 26

THE PUBLIC LAW PROTOCOL:[1] APPENDIX C

26.1 The Public Law Protocol (the Protocol) was first published in June 2003. It was a major, multi-disciplinary initiative. Its advisory committee, which reported in May 2003, was chaired by two Family Division High Court judges, Munby and Coleridge JJ. Its primary purpose was the elimination of unnecessary delay in public law proceedings relating to children. It set a guideline of 40 weeks for care cases under the Children Act 1989. In an introduction signed by the President of the Family Division, the Secretary of State for Constitutional Affairs and Lord Chancellor and the Secretary of State for Education and Skills, it was acknowledged that some cases would take more than 40 weeks, 'but many more cases should take less'.

26.2 Issued at the same time as the Protocol was a Practice Direction issued by the President with the concurrence of the Lord Chancellor entitled: Care Cases: Judicial Continuity and Judicial Case Management.[2]

26.3 Most of the Protocol need not concern you. It is aimed at lawyers and legal practitioners and lays down a detailed route map covering all the steps in care proceedings. As its title suggests, it places a strong emphasis on judicial case management and sets stringent time limits for the progress of every state of care proceedings.

26.4 An important part of the Protocol, however, is the Case Management Conference (CMC). This is a hearing attended by all the lawyers before the judge who is allocated to the case. The target time for it to take place is between 15 and 60 days after the care proceedings in question have been instituted. Its purpose, as expressed in the Protocol, is to ensure that 'a fair hearing of the proceedings takes place' and 'to time-table the proceedings so that the final hearing is completed within or before the recommended hearing window'. In practice this means ensuring that the issues in the case have been, or will be, properly addressed, and for present purposes deciding whether or not expert evidence is necessary and ensuring that, if it is, it is available.

26.5 The part of the Protocol which does directly concern you is Appendix C, which is reproduced below. As you will see, it sets out to deal comprehensively with your role in any care proceedings. It identifies the duties you owe to the court. It sets out a careful timetable for your instruction and identifies what should be in the letter of instruction sent to you. It goes on to deal with your report, questions which can be put to you in advance of the hearing, your meetings with fellow experts and the arrangements which should be made for you if you have to attend court.

26.6   The Protocol is currently being revised, and in due course it is intended that Appendix C will be incorporated into, and replaced by a Practice Direction which will form part of the new Public Law Outline and the Family Procedure Rules. In addition, Appendix C has been revised to take into account in particular what happened in the case of *Oldham MBC v W and others*.[3] The President and the Ministry of Justice kindly have agreed that the latest draft of the proposed Practice Direction can be included in this Handbook and it is, accordingly, set out in Appendix 11. What appears below, therefore, is Appendix C of the Protocol in its latest form. No doubt it will continue to be revised as time goes by. Nonetheless, neither the principles which underlie it, nor the matters with which it deals is likely to change and nothing in the proposed Practice Direction is in any way inconsistent either with Appendix C or the advice contained in this Handbook.

APPENDIX C
CODE OF GUIDANCE FOR EXPERT WITNESSES IN FAMILY PROCEEDINGS

Objective

The objective of this Code of Guidance is to provide the court with early information to enable it to determine whether it is necessary and/or practicable to ask an expert to assist the court:

– To identify, narrow and where possible agree the issues between the parties
– To provide an opinion about a question that is not within the skill and experience of the court
– To encourage the early identification of questions that need to be answered by an expert
– To encourage disclosure of full and frank information between the parties, the court and any expert instructed.

	Action	Party and timing
[1]	The duties of experts	
[1.1]	Overriding duty	
	An expert in family proceedings has an overriding duty to the court that takes precedence over any obligation to the person from whom he has received instructions or by whom he is paid.	
[1.2]	Particular duties	
	Among any other duties an expert may have, an expert shall have regard to the following duties:	
	• To assist the court in accordance with the overriding duty	
	• To provide an opinion that is independent of the party or parties instructing the expert	
	• To confine an opinion to matters material to the issues between the parties and in relation only to questions that are within the expert's expertise (skill and experience). If a question is put which falls outside that expertise the expert must say so	
	• In expressing an opinion take into consideration all of the material facts including any relevant factors arising from diverse cultural or religious contexts at the time the opinion is expressed, indicating the facts, literature and any other material that the expert has relied upon in forming an opinion	
	• To indicate whether the opinion is provisional (or qualified, as the case may be) and the reason for the qualification, identifying what further information is required to give an opinion without qualification	
	• Inform those instructing the expert without delay of any change in the opinion and the reason for the change.	

	Action	Party and timing	
[2] [2.1]	Preparation for the CMC Preliminary enquiries of the expert Not later than 10 days before the CMC the solicitor for the party proposing to instruct the expert (or lead solicitor/solicitor for the child if the instruction proposed is joint) shall approach the expert with the following information: • The nature of the proceedings and the issues likely to require determination by the court • The questions about which the expert is to be asked to give an opinion (including any diverse cultural or religious contexts) • When the court is to be asked to give permission for the instruction (if unusually permission has already been given the date and details of that permission) • Whether permission is asked of the court for the instruction of another expert in the same or any related field (ie to give an opinion on the same or related questions)	Solicitor instructing the expert	10 days before the CMC
	• The volume of reading which the expert will need to undertake • Whether or not (in an appropriate case) permission has been applied for or given for the expert to examine the child • Whether or not (in an appropriate case) it will be necessary for the expert to conduct interviews (and if so with whom) • The likely timetable of legal and social work steps • When the expert's opinion is likely to be required • Whether and if so what date has been fixed by the court for any hearing at which the expert may be required to give evidence (in particular the Final Hearing).		
[2.2]	Expert's response	Solicitor instructing	5 days before the

	Action	Party and timing	
		the expert	CMC
	Not later than 5 days before the CMC the solicitors intending to instruct the expert shall obtain the following information from the expert:		
	• That the work required is within the expert's expertise		
	• That the expert is available to do the relevant work within the suggested timescale		
	• When the expert is available to give evidence, the dates and/or times to avoid, and, where a hearing date has not been fixed, the amount of notice the expert will require to make arrangements to come to court without undue disruption to their normal clinical routines		
	• The cost, including hourly and global rates, and likely hours to be spent, of attending at experts/professionals meetings, attending court and writing the report (to include any examinations and interviews).		
[2.3]	Case Management Questionnaire	The party proposing to instruct the expert	Not later than 2 days before the CMC
	Any party who proposes to ask the court for permission to instruct an expert shall not later than 2 days before the CMC (or any hearing at which the application is to be made) file and serve a Case Management Questionnaire setting out the proposal to instruct the expert in the following detail:		
	• The name, discipline, qualifications and expertise of the expert (by way of CV where possible)		
	• The expert's availability to undertake the work		
	• The relevance of the expert evidence sought to be adduced to the issues in the proceedings and the specific questions upon which it is proposed the expert should give an opinion (including the relevance of any diverse cultural or religious contexts)		
	• The timetable for the report		

	Action	Party and timing	
	• The responsibility for instruction		
	• Whether or not the expert evidence can properly be obtained by the joint instruction of the expert by two or more of the parties		
	• Whether the expert evidence can properly be obtained by only one party (eg on behalf of the child)		
	• Whether it is necessary for more than one expert in the same discipline to be instructed by more than one party		
	• Why the expert evidence proposed cannot be given by social services undertaking a core assessment or by the guardian in accordance with their different statutory duties		
	• The likely cost of the report on both an hourly and global basis		
	• The proposed apportionment of costs of jointly instructed experts as between the LA and the publicly funded parties.		
[2.4]	Draft order for the CMC Any party proposing to instruct an expert shall in the draft order submitted at the CMC request the court to give directions (among any others) as to the following: • The party who is to be responsible for drafting the letter of instruction and providing the documents to the expert • The issues identified by the court and the questions about which the expert is to give an opinion • The timetable within which the report is to be prepared, filed and served • The disclosure of the report to the parties and to any other expert • The conduct of an experts' discussion • The preparation of a statement of agreement and disagreement by the experts following an experts'	Any party	Not later than 2 days before the CMC

	Action	**Party and timing**	
	discussion • The attendance of the expert at the Final Hearing unless agreement is reached at or before the PHR about the opinions given by the expert.		
[3] [3.1]	Letter of Instruction The solicitor instructing the expert shall within 5 days of the CMC prepare (agree with the other parties where appropriate) file and serve a letter of instruction to the expert which shall: • Set out the context in which the expert's opinion is sought (including any diverse ethnic, cultural, religious or linguistic contexts) • Define carefully the specific questions the expert is required to answer ensuring: – that they are within the ambit of the expert's area of expertise and – that they do not contain unnecessary or irrelevant detail – that the questions addressed to the expert are kept to a manageable number and are clear, focused and direct – that the questions reflect what the expert has been requested to do by the court • List the documentation provided or provide for the expert an indexed and paginated bundle which shall include: – a copy of the order (or those parts of the order) which gives permission for the instruction of the expert immediately the order becomes available – an agreed list of essential reading – all new documentation when it is filed and regular updates to the list of documents provided or to the index to the paginated bundle – a copy of this code of guidance and of the Protocol	Solicitor instructing the expert	Within 5 days of the CMC
	• Identify the relevant lay and		

	Action	Party and timing	
	professional people concerned with the proceedings (eg the treating clinicians) and inform the expert of his/her right to talk to the other professionals provided an accurate record is made of the discussion		
	• Identify any other expert instructed in the proceedings and advise the expert of his/her right to talk to the other experts provided an accurate record is made of the discussion		
	• Define the contractual basis upon which the expert is retained and in particular the funding mechanism including how much the expert will be paid (an hourly rate and overall estimate should already have been obtained) when the expert will be paid, and what limitation there might be on the amount the expert can charge for the work which he/she will have to do. There should also be a brief explanation of the 'detailed assessment process' in cases proceeding in the care centre or the High Court which are not subject to a high cost case contract		
	• In default of agreement the format of the Letter of Instruction shall be determined by the court, which may determine the issue upon written application with representations from each party.		
[4] [4.1]	The expert's report Content of the report The expert's report shall be addressed to the court and shall: • Give details of the expert's qualifications and experience • Contain a statement setting out the substance of all material instructions (whether written or oral) summarising the facts stated and instructions given to the expert which are material to the conclusions and opinions expressed in the report • Give details of any literature or other research material upon which the expert has relied in giving an opinion	The expert	In accordance with the court's timetable

	Action	Party and timing	
	• State who carried out any test, examination or interview which the expert has used for the report and whether or not the test, examination or interview has been carried out under the expert's supervision • Give details of the qualifications of any person who carried out the test, examination or interview • Where there is a range of opinion on the question to be answered by the expert: – summarise the range of opinion and – give reasons for the opinion expressed • Contain a summary of the expert's conclusions and opinions • Contain a statement that the expert understands his duty to the court and has complied with that duty • Where appropriate be verified by a statement of truth.		
[4.2]	Supplementary questions Any party wishing to ask supplementary questions of an expert for the purpose of clarifying the expert's report must put those questions in writing to the parties not later than 5 days after receipt of the report. Only those questions that are agreed by the parties or in default of agreement approved by the court may be put to the expert. The court may determine the issue upon written application with representations from each party.	Any party	Within 5 days of the receipt of the report
[5] [5.1]	Experts' discussion (meeting) Purpose The court will give directions for the experts to meet or communicate: • To identify and narrow the issues in the case • To reach agreement on the expert questions • To identify the reasons for	The court	at the CMC

	Action	Party and timing	
	disagreement on any expert question and to identify what if any action needs to be taken to resolve any outstanding disagreement/question		
	• To obtain elucidation or amplification of relevant evidence in order to assist the court to determine the issues		
	• To limit, wherever possible, the need for experts to attend court to give oral evidence.		
[5.2]	The arrangements for a discussion/meeting In accordance with the directions given by the court at the CMC, the solicitor for the child or such other professional who is given the responsibility by the court shall make arrangements for there to be a discussion between the experts within 10 days of the filing of the experts' reports. The following matters should be considered: • Where permission has been given for the instruction of experts from different disciplines a global discussion may be held relating to those questions that concern all or most of them • Separate discussions may have to be held among experts from the same or related disciplines but care should be taken to ensure that the discussions complement each other so that related questions are discussed by all relevant experts • 7 days prior to a discussion or meeting the solicitor for the child or other nominated professional should formulate an agenda to include a list of the questions for consideration. This may usefully take the form of a list of questions to be circulated among the other parties in advance. The agenda should comprise all questions that each party wishes the experts to consider. The agenda and list of questions should be sent to each of the experts not later than 2 days before the discussion	Child's solicitor	Within 10 days of the filing of the experts' reports
	• The discussion should usually be chaired by the child's solicitor or in		

	Action	**Party and timing**	
	exceptional cases where the parties have applied to the court at the CMC, by an independent professional identified by the parties or the court. In complex medical cases it may be necessary for the discussion to be jointly chaired by an expert. A minute must be taken of the questions answered by the experts, and a Statement of Agreement and Disagreement must be prepared which should be agreed and signed by each of the experts who participated in the discussion. The statement should be served and filed not later than 5 days after the discussion has taken place • Consideration should be given in each case to whether some or all of the experts participate by telephone conference or video link to ensure that minimum disruption is caused to clinical schedules.		
[5.3]	Positions of the parties Where any party refuses to be bound by an agreement that has been reached at an experts' discussion that party must inform the court at or before the PHR of the reasons for refusing to accept the agreement.	Any party	At the PHR
[5.4]	Professionals meetings In proceedings where the court gives a direction that a professionals meeting shall take place between the LA and any relevant named professionals for the purpose of providing assistance to the LA in the formulation of plans and proposals for the child, the meeting shall be arranged, chaired and minuted in accordance with directions given by the court.		
[6] [6.1]	Arranging for the expert to attend court Preparation The party who is responsible for the instruction of an expert witness shall ensure: • That a date and time is fixed for the court to hear the expert's	Every party responsible for the instruction of an expert	By the PHR

	Action	Party and timing	
	evidence that is, if possible, convenient to the expert and that the fixture is made substantially in advance of the Final Hearing and no later than at the PHR (ie no later than 2 weeks before the Final Hearing) • That if the expert's oral evidence is not required the expert is notified as soon as possible • That the witness template accurately indicates how long the expert is likely to be giving evidence, in order to avoid the inconvenience of the expert being delayed at court.		
[6.2]	All parties shall ensure • That where expert witnesses are to be called the advocates attending the PHR have identified at the advocates meeting the issues which the experts are to address • That wherever possible a logical sequence to the evidence is arranged with experts of the same discipline giving evidence on the same day(s) • That at the PHR the court is informed of any circumstance where all experts agree but a party nevertheless does not accept the agreed opinion so that directions can be given for the proper consideration of the experts' evidence and the parties reasons for not accepting the same • That in the exceptional case the court is informed of the need for a witness summons.	All parties	At the PHR
[7] [7.1]	Post hearing action Within 10 days of the Final Hearing the solicitor instructing the expert should provide feedback to the expert by way of a letter informing the expert of the outcome of the case, and the use made by the court of the expert's opinion. Where the court directs that a copy of the transcript can be sent to the expert, the solicitor instructing the expert should obtain the transcript within 10 days of the Final Hearing.	Solicitor instructing the expert	Within 10 days of the Final Hearing

26.7   Although the Protocol relates to what are called 'public law' proceedings, the principles applicable to expert evidence apply equally to private law proceedings under the Children Act 1989.[4]

NOTES

[1]   Its full title is the *Protocol for Judicial Case Management in Public Law Children Act cases.* It is to be found in a number of places – eg [2003] 2 FLR 719.

[2]   [2003] 2 FLR 798.

[3]   [2005] EWCA Civ 1247; and [2007] EWHC 136 (Fam). The issues which arose in this case are discussed in more detail in Chapter 32.

[4]   For the distinction between public law and private law proceedings, see Chapter 3.

Chapter 27

THE FAMILY JUSTICE COUNCIL

Stephen Cobb QC

27.1   Family Justice has always been multi-disciplinary and practitioners from its many disciplines campaigned for years for an authoritative inter-disciplinary body which could monitor the system, discuss important problems and make recommendations for change and improvement. The Family Justice Council (FJC) thus has its origins in a number of interdisciplinary initiatives,[1] although it was not finally established until 2004.

27.2   The overall aim of the FJC is to facilitate the delivery of better and quicker outcomes for families and children who use the family justice system. Its primary role, however, is to promote an inter-disciplinary approach to family justice. Through consultation and research, it aims to monitor how effectively the system delivers the service which the public needs and to advise government on necessary reforms and improvements. Its terms of reference are set out in Appendix 2.

27.3   The FJC is chaired by the President of the Family Division. It has 30 members, of whom 17 are appointed.[2] From your perspective, you should note that amongst the appointed members are:

- a Consultant Paediatrician
- a Child Mental Health Specialist (Consultant child and adolescent psychiatrist)
- a member appointed specifically to represent the views of the child
- a member appointed specifically to represent the interests of parents.

27.4   The full list of the professional disciplines represented on the FJC and the current appointed members is available on www.family-justice-council.org.uk (see generally on the website below).

27.5   The Council's detailed work is carried out within three main committees, namely:

- Children in Safeguarding Proceedings Committee (principally concerned with issues which arise in 'care' and public law proceedings)

- Children in Families Committee (principally concerned with 'private' law proceedings)
- Money and Property Committee (principally concerned with ancillary relief and related proceedings).

27.6 There are other important committees and working groups whose work feeds into each of the main committees. These committees and working groups are convened specifically to address:

- Experts
- Domestic Violence
- The Voice of the Child
- Diversity
- Transparency
- Education and Training
- Executive.

The committees, other than the Executive Committee, contain a number of co-opted members who are experts in relevant fields but who are not members of the main council.

WHAT ARE THE LOCAL FAMILY JUSTICE COUNCILS AND WHAT CAN THEY DO FOR YOU?

27.7 The Family Justice Council (FJC) has established a network of local FJCs regionally. Local FJCs have been established in 40 areas around the country. The composition of the local FJCs is intended broadly to mirror the appointed membership of the FJC – that is to say, representatives from all of the key stakeholders in the family justice system, including, of course, representatives specialising in the fields of child health and child mental health.

27.8 Each local FJC has a 'sponsor' member of the main council to facilitate the links between the two.

27.9 If you would like to know which member of the national council sponsors the local FJC in your area, you can contact the FJC secretariat on fjc@courtservice.gsi.gov.uk.

27.10 If you are interested in the work of the local FJC in your area, (and/or wish to gain greater understanding of inter-disciplinary initiatives going on in your area under the auspices of the FJC) you should contact the FJC Secretariat who will put you in touch with the local administrator. Alternatively, you can contact the representative in your field on the local Council.

THE EXPERTS COMMITTEE OF THE FJC

27.11 At the time of writing, there are 19 members of the Experts Committee. Six are drawn from the FJC and thirteen are co-opted to the Committee. There are representatives drawn from many relevant disciplines of medical expertise, together with representation from CAFCASS,[3] the Ministry of Justice and the General Medical Council. The full list of members of the Experts Committee at the time of writing also appears in Appendix 2.

27.12 The Experts Committee meets approximately four times per year. The meetings provide a forum for discussion of issues relevant to expert evidence in the family courts. The Sub-Committee has concentrated in its early years of its formation on examining:

- The quality of experts giving evidence in the courts, including issues relating to accreditation and qualification
- The supply of experts, with a view to encouraging doctors to undertake medico-legal work
- Principles of good practice in preparing and delivering expert opinions
- Inter-disciplinary training programmes and other initiatives nationally and regionally (this followed an extensive mapping exercise in which we considered inter-disciplinary activity around the country)
- Funding of expert evidence
- The inter-relation between judicial analysis of expert opinion, and complaints to professional bodies
- Publication of judgments and the implications of publicity for experts
- And recently, of course, the report of the Chief Medical Officer (*Bearing Good Witness*) and the Sub-Committee's response to the recommendations included within it.

27.13 While the FJC cannot become involved in considering or commenting on individual cases, if you would like the Experts Committee to consider issues of practice or principle which arise, or have arisen, in the course of your engagement with the family justice system, then you should contact the FJC secretariat (and/or the expert on the Committee whose discipline would be relevant) and ask for the matter to be considered.

Promotion of inter-disciplinary activity

27.14 If you are interested in observing a court in action as a spectator, then you should consider taking up a 'mini-pupillage'. Do not be put off by the name, which derives from the fact that before they can take a brief, barristers have to be the 'pupil' of a more senior barrister. What the 'mini-pupillage' scheme is designed to do is to enable you to spend a day or more sitting with a specialist family judge and observing family proceedings in action.

27.15 The scheme has been in operation since 1999.[4] Initially, it was administered from the Royal Courts of Justice but as it developed, so it has been rolled out throughout the country. The FJC strongly promotes (and has taken some ownership of) the scheme.

27.16 As already stated, the scheme is designed to introduce Specialist Registrars and Consultants to the work of the court. In particular, the scheme aims to give Specialist Registrars and Consultants:

- experience of the court environment
- assistance in preparing them for the presenting oral and written evidence in court
- a clearer understanding of the legal perspectives
- an opportunity to discuss issues arising (from individual cases observed and generally) in fulfilling the role of an expert witness.

27.17 Normally, as stated above, a 'mini-pupillage' involves spending a day or more with a specialist family judge. If you would be interested in doing this, you should contact the FJC Secretariat for the High Court in London, your local FJC (see Appendix 2) or the Designated Family Judge for the court centre in the region in which you work.[5] Every effort should be made locally to ensure that the judge with whom you sit will be hearing a case which is relevant to your specialty on the day or days when you come to sit in, although in the smaller centres, this cannot be guaranteed.

27.18 Mini-pupillage schemes are also available with barristers through the Family Law Bar Association. These can be arranged by contacting the Administrator of the Family Law Bar Association at the Bar Council (currently, Carol Harris telephone 020 7242 1289: charris@barcouncil.org.uk). The Administrator will put you in touch with the barrister member of the FLBA Committee specifically designated to deal with inter-disciplinary training (a post on the FLBA which has been created at the instigation of the FJC).

27.19 The Child & Adolescent Psychiatry Specialist Advisory Sub-Committee (CAPSAC) advises the Specialist Training Committee (STC) of the Royal College of Psychiatrists on matters relating to training in child and adolescent psychiatry. A list of the Regional CAPSAC scheme co-ordinators / Training Program Directors is available from your local FJC. We encourage you to contact these scheme co-ordinators in order to stimulate inter-disciplinary training in the field of psychiatry.

THE FJC WEBSITE

27.20 The FJC has a website at www.family-justice-council.org.uk. The FJC publishes on the website the minutes of meetings, its written responses to Government consultations, other papers and reports.

27.21 On the website, you will find the Guide to the Family Justice System which was written and designed by members of the Council. Although this guide is primarily designed to help families and young people find their way around the family justice system and access the services provided to deal with relationship breakdown and its consequences, it nonetheless provides a useful guide for all.

27.22 You will also find the CAFCASS Research Digest (issued quarterly between 2002 and 2006) published on the Family Justice Council website. The Family Justice Council is keen to promote the development of knowledge and understanding of the working of the Family Justice System, and is keen to make research about family justice and other related issues more widely available. Other links to research reports where they are available on the web is also provided.

AN EXAMPLE OF THE EXPERTS COMMITTEE'S WORK: QUESTIONS FOR EXPERT WITNESSES

27.23 Concern expressed among the medical experts about the lack of focus and discipline in the drafting and submission of questions to the experts caused the Experts Committee to consider and draft 'standard' questions for experts to be used (with necessary adaptation) in children's cases. These are also contained in Appendix 2. These questions attracted approval in the review of the Judicial Case Management Protocol.

HOW DO YOU CONTACT THE FJC?

27.24 If you have any questions about the operation of the FJC or the local FJC in your area, or otherwise wish to make contact with the secretariat of the FJC, you should make contact in one of the ways identified below:

fjc@courtservice.gsi.gov.uk

or at

Family Justice Council
E201 East Block
Royal Courts of Justice
Strand
London
WC2A 2LL

Telephone: +44 (0)20 7947 7333/7974/7950

Fax: +44 (0)20 7947 7875

SUMMARY

27.25 The creation of the FJC is a significant development in family justice. It provides an interdisciplinary forum which addresses all the various aspects of the system. Its objective is to promote good practice. Its Experts Committee aims to encourage appropriately qualified doctors to become expert witnesses. It should also provide a forum in which you can raise anxieties you have or difficulties which you have encountered.

NOTES

1   Following the implementation of the Children Act 1989 in October 1989, the Children Act Advisory Committee was given a five year life and produced many good ideas. Its dissolution in 1996 acutely pointed up the need for a national interdisciplinary body. The National Council for Family Proceedings carried the banner for a time, as did the President of the Family Division's Interdisciplinary Committee, an ad hoc body which emerged after the first of what turned out to be a succession of successful biennial conferences held at Dartington Hall in September 1995, the results of which were published by Jordans Publishing. The first of these, published under the title *Rooted Sorrows*, which addressed psychoanalytic perspective on child protection, therapy and treatment, is still in print. However, the need for a body supported and sponsored by government was increasingly recognised and the creation of one 'overarching' public body to support effective inter-agency co-operation in the family justice system had been the key recommendation of the consultation paper published in March 2002 entitled 'Promoting Inter-Agency Working in the Family Justice System'. The 2002 Consultation paper further recommended that the Council should be supported by a series of specialist sub-committees and should have direct links with local court based groups – a structure designed to ensure that there is a constructive dialogue between national bodies and local practitioners.

2   Appointment was by open competition (application, and interview, with references) in accordance with the Code of Practice for appointment to public bodies. There are a number of ex-officio members drawn from the Government departments and other agencies (including The Children and Family Court Advisory and Support Service (CAFCASS), CAFCASS Cymru, Children's Commissioners for England and for Wales, the Legal Services Commission, Ministry of Justice, DfES, Home Office, The Court Service, the Association of Chief Police Officers and FCO).

3   The Children and Family Court Advisory and Support Service, established in 2001 to replace the Court Welfare Service, Guardian panels and the role of the Official Solicitor as the guardian of children in family proceedings. See also Appendix 10.

4   The President's Interdisciplinary Committee, in co-operation with the Royal College of Psychiatrists and the Royal College of Paediatrics and Child Health, launched this mini-pupillage scheme for specialist registrars and consultants.

5   Each care centre is headed by a 'designated' family judge (DFJ). This is a circuit judge who specialises in family work and is responsible for its allocation in the care centre. Many DFJs also chair their local FJCs and are generally active in interdisciplinary activities. A list of DFJs is at Appendix 3.

Chapter 28

THE RELEVANCE OF THE HUMAN RIGHTS ACT 1998 (HRA 1998) AND THE EUROPEAN CONVENTION ON HUMAN RIGHTS (ECHR)

28.1 ECHR was incorporated into English Law by the HRA 1998, which came into force on 2 October 2000. Most of the cases arising in family proceedings since that date engage ECHR Article 6 (the right to a fair trial) and ECHR Article 8 (the right to respect for private and family life). Where family proceedings are pending, the courts have discouraged lawyers from taking separate proceedings to argue points under the HRA 1998 and ECHR. The courts have taken the view that most ECHR points can be decided within the family proceedings themselves. The courts decided very early on that the Children Act 1989 in general was HRA compliant.

28.2 Whilst the HRA 1998 and ECHR are both very important and whilst you should, of course, be fully aware of the terms in particular of ECHR Articles 6 and 8,[1] it is unlikely that either the HRA 1998 or ECHR will impinge on your work as an expert witness. This is because procedural fairness is essentially a matter for the court, not for you, and because, in practice, the relevance of ECHR Article 8 in family proceedings is the need for the court to balance the respective rights of the adults and the children concerned and to seek to achieve a result which is in the best interests of the child. Once again, this is a matter which is ultimately for the court and not usually for you. If you are asked for your opinion about what is in the best interests of a particular child and if the answer to that question is within the area of your expertise, you should answer it by reference to the child's welfare, not by reference to the HRA 1998 or ECHR.

28.3 In short, therefore, the Children Act 1989 and the various court procedures which it involves are HRA compliant and you should resist any invitation to become involved in arguments under either HRA 1998 or ECHR.

SUMMARY

28.4 Important as they may be in terms of the court process, the Human Rights Act 1998 and European Convention on Human Rights are unlikely to impinge on your work as an expert witness.

NOTES

[1]   The relevant part of Article 6.1 for present purposes reads: 'In the determination of his civil rights and obligations ... everyone is entitled to a fair and public hearing within a reasonable time by an independent and impartial tribunal established by law. Judgment shall be pronounced publicly but the press and public may be excluded from all or part of the trial ... where the interests of juveniles or the protection of the private life of the parties so require, or to the extent strictly necessary in the opinion of the court in special circumstances where publicity would prejudice the interests of justice'. You should note that the practice in England and Wales of hearing family cases in private and giving judgments in private with the press excluded has been upheld in the European Court of Human Rights: see *B v United Kingdom*; *P v United Kingdom* [2001] 2 FLR 261 and Chapter 35.

ECHR Article 8.1 reads: 'Everyone has the right to respect for his private and family life, his home and his correspondence'. Article 8.2 reads: 'There shall be no interference by a public authority with the exercise of this right except such as is in accordance with the law and is necessary in a democratic society ... for the protection of health or morals, or for the protection of the rights and freedoms of others'.

Chapter 29

WHICH EXPERT? PSYCHIATRIST OR PSYCHOLOGIST?

29.1 This chapter has been included because it has been suggested that it would be helpful to mental health professionals to have an understanding of how the courts view psychiatry and psychology and what factors influence the court in deciding which branch of expertise to call upon in the individual case. What follows is necessarily, therefore, both general and, to a degree, subjective.[1]

29.2 In most cases of physical abuse, of course, the question 'which expert' answers itself and is dependent upon the specific injury or injuries suffered by the child. As medical science itself becomes more specialised and sophisticated, so do the categories of medical expert called upon to advise the court in relation to children's injuries.

29.3 This question 'which expert' thus usually only arises in an acute form when the issue for the court is whether or not it needs assistance in its assessment of a child or carer's mental health, or where the question is one of the human relationships both between the adults themselves and between the adults and their children. In practical terms, the question usually boils down to an analysis of the relationship between parents and their children and the capacity of a given individual to be a competent parent. In such cases, there is scope for legitimate debate. Should the expert to be engaged be a psychiatrist (adult, forensic or child and adolescent) or should the expert be a psychologist (child or adult)?[2]

29.4 In practice, of course, the choice of expert in this field is often determined by local resources. It is, however, I hope useful for experts to understand how the legal profession differentiates between psychiatry and psychology.

29.5 Judges generally perceive psychiatry as the study and medical treatment of diseases of the mind. Evidence from an adult psychiatrist is, therefore, particularly relevant where one of the adult parties suffers from, or is alleged to suffer from, an identifiable disease of the mind, or where children have been caused serious emotional damage by the manner in which they have been treated.

29.6 Child and Adolescent psychiatry is, of course, a recognised specialism within psychiatry itself and child psychiatrists can give evidence, not only of mental illness in children and young people, but the emotional consequences on children of abuse, notably sexual abuse and domestic violence.[3] Some child and adolescent psychiatrists have also become expert both at interviewing and diagnosing children who are alleged to have been sexually abused. They are thus able to advise, not just about whether or not a particular interview with a child has been properly conducted, but as to whether or not the child has in fact been sexually abused.[4]

29.7   Psychology is perceived by lawyers as distinct from psychiatry, although there are some obvious overlaps. Psychologists are rarely medically qualified. Lawyers see psychology as the study of the human personality and behaviour. Thus a psychologist is likely to be instructed to undertake an assessment of one or both of the parents and, most commonly, to assess their capacity to care for their children.

29.8   Child psychology is, of course, a recognised specialism within psychology, and there are many child psychologists who are equally capable of advising the court, for example, on child development, the nature and strength of the relationship between children and their parents, whether or not a child has been the victim of sexual abuse and the likely emotional consequences of abuse and neglect.

29.9   Both adult and child and adolescent psychiatrists therefore tend to be instructed as expert witnesses either (in the case of the former) when it is alleged that one or more of the parties is suffering from a mental illness or (in relation to children) where the suggestion is that a child has been sexually abused or otherwise significantly harmed emotionally by parental behaviour (such as domestic violence or neglect). Child psychiatrists with a detailed knowledge of child development are also able to give evidence of the relationship between children and their parents and the likely risks to those children if they are allowed either to remain in or are returned to the care of their parents. Plainly, however, a competent child psychologist can cover much of the same ground.

29.10   In the assessment of parental capacity to care for children there is also an overlap with social work. In most, if not every care case, the local authority will undertake a core assessment of the family and reach a conclusion about the family's dynamics and the capacity of the parents to care for their children. That process may be a multi-disciplinary process involving local CAMHS personnel. A psychological assessment of the family is usually only necessary where the core assessment is challenged. A psychiatric assessment is likely to be more focused on a specific mental health issue or issues.

29.11   As is made clear in Chapter 30, whilst psychometric testing has a place in the overall assessment of an individual's personality and capacity, it should not be used as the basis for an opinion on adult credibility.

29.12   As a broad generalisation, there seem to be more psychologists available to give expert evidence than psychiatrists. Whatever your discipline, the same principles apply. You must ask yourself whether or not the task which the court is setting you is properly within the area of your expertise. If you do not think it is, you should refuse to accept the instructions to act.

NOTES

[1]   For a full and helpful discussion of the subject, see Elizabeth Walsh: *Working in the Family Justice System*, Family Law, 2nd edition pp 92–103.

[2]   I am not overlooking the fact that there are some excellent independent social work experts who both deserve and are accorded expert status. The core social work assessment in any case is, however, a matter for the local authority social workers and the need for analysis and comment on the social work aspects of care cases can usually be left to the children's guardian. This chapter does not, therefore, address experts in social work, although plainly there are cases (and individuals who are well known locally) in which such evidence is required.

[3]   Perhaps the best and most influential example is the report prepared by two psychiatrists for the Court of Appeal in the cases of *Re L, V, M and H (Contact domestic Violence)* [2000] EWCA Civ 194. The report itself is published in *Family Law* for 2000 (Vol 30 at page 615).

[4]   This is a controversial area, as the Report of the Inquiry into Child Abuse in Cleveland 1987 (Cm 412) demonstrated. However, in the case of *Re M and R (Child Abuse: Evidence)* [1996] 2 FLR 195, the Court of Appeal decided that, by reason of section 3 of the Civil Evidence Act 1972, experts could give evidence on any matter within the area of their expertise, including the very factual question which the court itself had to decide. Thus, if a child psychiatrist was competent to give evidence on the credibility of a child when relating allegations of sexual abuse, that evidence was admissible, although the decision as to whether or not the child had been sexually abused remained that of the judge. It is to be noted, however, that this rule does not extend to adult credibility. Whether or not an adult is telling the truth is not a matter for expert evidence, particularly psychometric testing: see Chapters 7 and 30.

Chapter 30

RELIANCE ON PSYCHOMETRIC TESTING

30.1   Psychometric testing is plainly an important tool for the psychologist who is making an assessment of an individual's personality and characteristics – usually in the context of an assessment of that person's capacity to care for children. Nothing in what follows is intended to devalue its use in such contexts, although psychologists who use it must be prepared to be challenged over their methodology in some cases.[1]

30.2   As stated earlier in Chapter 7, questions of adult witness credibility (in other words: 'is a witness telling the truth?') are matters of fact to be decided by the judge. They are not matters on which you advise the judge.

30.3   In two recent cases,[2] the Court of Appeal has made it clear that it does not regard psychometric testing as having any place in cases where adult witness credibility is in issue.

30.4   In the first of the two cases, the judge had placed considerable reliance on the evidence of a clinical psychologist who had interviewed the mother of the child concerned and administered a personality test which included a 'lie scale' which measured 'the subject's willingness to distort her responses in order to create a good impression'. He also required the mother to complete a 'child abuse potential inventory'. He stated in his report: 'The one conclusion it is safe to draw from (her) responses on the personality questionnaires is her lack of candour and her strong wish to portray herself in the most favourable light'. However, the psychologist later qualified his conclusions.

30.5   All three judges in the Court of Appeal were critical of the judge's reliance on the personality tests. Scott Baker LJ said:[3] 'I do not feel that psychometric testing ordinarily has any place in cases of this kind. It is for the judge to evaluate the facts and assess questions of credibility. He sees the witnesses give evidence and has an overview of the whole picture of the case. It is important that expert witnesses or purported experts should not trespass into his field of responsibility'. Arden LJ said[4] that if the judge was (exceptionally) minded to rely on the results of the personality tests, he had first to assess their validity, both generally and for the purpose of the case. Ward LJ, who gave the leading judgment in the case, said he would go so far as to say that personality tests were likely to obfuscate the judicial process rather than assist it. Judges assessed credibility day in and day out. They did not need personality tests to assist then and were 'probably far better off without them'. Similar sentiments were expressed by the Court of Appeal in *Re L*.[5]

30.6   If, therefore, you are a psychologist who is instructed to make an assessment of a parent or other adult in the case, you should think very carefully indeed before using psychometric testing as a basis for a conclusion that the person who is the subject of the tests is being truthful in relation to a particular event.

SUMMARY

30.7   Psychometric testing should not be used in reports for court proceedings to found an opinion about whether or not the person being assessed is telling the truth about a particular incident.

NOTES

1   See, for example, *Re L (children)* [2006] EWCA Civ 1282 in which adverse comment was made in the Court of Appeal about a psychologist's lengthy interview with a man who had learning difficulties.
2   *Re S (Care: Parenting Skills: Personality Tests)* [2004] EWCA Civ 1029; *Re L* (above).
3   *Re S* at paragraph 71.
4   Ibid, at paragraph 67.
5   See, in particular, paragraphs 23–25 (per Wilson LJ) and paragraph 69 (per Wall LJ).

Chapter 31

ANONYMOUS OR PARTIAL INSTRUCTIONS

ANONYMOUS INSTRUCTIONS

31.1 You should never accept anonymous instructions. In every case in which you are asked to give an opinion, you should make sure that the court has either given permission for you (or an expert in your discipline) to be instructed or that the court is going to be asked for that permission. Before starting work, you should always see a copy of the court order in which permission for you to act has been given. If you are not sent it with your instructions, ask to see it. Always make sure that what you are being asked to do is both within the area of your expertise and the remit given to you by the court.

31.2 *Re A (Family Proceedings: Expert Witness)*[1] is a salutary reminder of how things should not be done. There were long standing private law proceedings between parents about their children. The father was having supervised contact at a family centre and the court had given permission for the papers to be disclosed to the centre to enable it to make an assessment of the family and the needs of the children. The centre produced two reports from a multi-disciplinary team comprising three therapists and two consultant psychiatrists. Unbeknown to the children's mother and the family centre, the father's solicitors sent a videotape which the father had taken of his contact with the children (and which he had stated he had no intention of using in court) to a clinical psychologist. The solicitors asked him to write a report on the quality of the father's interaction with the children and the desirability of contact being maintained. Permission had not been obtained from the court for the expert to report.

31.3 The first letter of instruction to the psychologist made no reference to the ongoing proceedings between the parents. It simply enclosed the video and asked ten questions about it. When the psychologist requested further information, he was sent a detailed and, in places, highly tendentious letter. This letter was written in an anonymised form and set out the history of the case, including the fact of the court proceedings. The second letter had been sent to counsel to approve. Assuming that permission had been given by the court for him to report, the psychologist duly did so.

31.4   The father exhibited the report to his statement in the proceedings. His solicitors accepted that the court had not given permission for the instruction of the psychologist and that as a result they were personally responsible for his fees. They sought to justify their conduct on the grounds that they had not disclosed any court papers and the fact that instructions had been given anonymously meant that there had been no breach of the Family Proceedings Rules.

31.5   The psychologist explained to the court that it was not unusual for him to receive anonymous instructions, particularly in relation to Asian families. He thought he would offend solicitors and could be criticised as questioning their professional integrity if he were to ask explicitly whether or not they had the court's permission to instruct him.

The need for transparency

31.6   The attitude of the father's lawyers and the psychologist in this case demonstrated some profound misunderstandings. The essence of case management in proceedings relating to children is that the process should be transparent and that each party should know the case that party has to meet. It is for the court to decide what evidence should and should not be obtained and quite wrong for one party to commission a report from an expert about which the other party knows nothing.

31.7   It is equally impermissible for a solicitor to conceal from the other parties to the case the fact that, although permission has been given to instruct a particular expert, the expert in question has declined to accept instructions.[2]

31.8   The psychologist in this case should not have accepted anonymous instructions. As an expert witness, you are entitled to know, and indeed must know, the terms of the court order which defines your involvement and the purpose for which you have been instructed. You must not simply 'assume' that the solicitors instructing you have the court's permission to do so. Any competent solicitor will volunteer the information and would expect you both to ask about it and to want to see a copy of the court order. There can be no offence in making these necessary enquiries.

PARTIAL INSTRUCTIONS

31.9   By this I mean instructions to undertake one particular task. There are circumstances in which this is wholly appropriate. For example, if you are asked to analyse a particular hair sample and this is your area of expertise you do not need to know anything very much about the case, apart from the fact that the court has made a direction that you be provided with a sample for analysis.

There are many other single issues (usually purely scientific) which do not require the expert involved to be shown the court papers or to read deeply into the case. Nonetheless, the important point remains. If you cannot properly advise without receiving more information, always ask for it.

31.10 A more difficult issue arises if you are asked to comment on the work done by another expert in the case, particularly if the purpose for which you are asked to comment is to provide counsel who is to cross-examine the expert in question with material upon which to do so.

31.11 Although 'never' is a dangerous word to use in proceedings relating to children, the court should, I think, be very cautious about making any such order and you should be equally cautious about accepting partial instructions of this type. The dangers are obvious. If the only document you are allowed to see is your colleague's report, your knowledge of the case is inevitably circumscribed and you may be led into making false assumptions by your lack of knowledge of the case.

31.12 It must be acknowledged, however, that there are cases in which it is appropriate for the papers to be shown to a second expert with a view to that expert providing a critique of a colleague's work. If you are asked to do this, you should only accept the instructions if you feel you have sufficient information upon which to express a proper opinion – that is, one with which you can be professionally satisfied.

SUMMARY

31.13 You should never accept anonymous instructions. You should always ask to see the terms of the court order permitting your involvement and you should always be clear about your remit. You will not cause offence by making proper inquiries. It is contrary to good practice for solicitors to seek to avoid the need to seek the court's permission by sending you anonymous instructions.

31.14 If you are given partial instructions, for example to provide a critique of a colleague's work in the case, you should only accept those instructions if you feel you have sufficient information upon which to express a proper opinion.

NOTES

1   [2001] 1 FLR 723. Most family cases which pre-date BAILII unfortunately have no neutral citation number.
2   See *Re V (Care Proceedings: Human Rights Claims)* [2004] EWCA Civ 54 at paragraphs 57–69 and 122.

Chapter 32

THE DANGERS OF BEING THE SINGLE EXPERT

32.1 You have a particular responsibility if you are the only expert instructed in a particular discipline in a case. If your opinion is pivotal, and if other experts from different disciplines defer to you, the consequences for the child and the family can be devastating if you are wrong.

32.2 If you are the sole expert in these circumstances, and if you feel the burden of responsibility is too great, you should not hesitate to ask the solicitor instructing you to invite the judge to give permission for one of the parties in the case adversely affected by your opinion to seek a second opinion from a different but equally qualified expert. This will not be perceived by the court as a sign of weakness or as an indication that your opinion is unsound.

32.3 There are cases where fairness to the parties requires the court to order a second opinion and you should not feel inhibited in suggesting that course if you think it appropriate. You should always remember that the court's objective is to reach the result which is in the best interests of the child. Children's interests are not served if the court reaches the wrong result on the basis of expert evidence, given in good faith, but which turns out to be wrong.

32.4 However, the fact that you are the only expert in a particular discipline in the case is not an automatic reason for one of the parties to obtain a second opinion. It all depends on the circumstances of the particular case. The more specialised the field, the more significant your opinion is likely to be. The court needs, in every case, to decide carefully what evidence is required and there are many cases in which a single, jointly instructed expert is appropriate.[1]

32.5 *W v Oldham MBC*[2] is a paradigm example of the type of miscarriage of justice which can occur where there is a single expert on a critical part of the case, to whose opinion the other doctors in the case defer, and where the court initially refuses to permit a second opinion.

32.6 The facts of *W v Oldham MBC* were that on 8 April 2005, an experienced and highly competent judge decided that a child, identified only by the initial K, had suffered non-accidental head injuries, probably caused by a single shaking episode and inflicted by one of his parents. The threshold criteria under section 31 of the Children Act 1989 were, accordingly, satisfied.

32.7 In reaching that conclusion, the judge had relied on the evidence of a single expert in the field of paediatric neuroradiology, who had concluded that the injuries suffered by the child were probably non-accidental. On two occasions, the judge refused the parents' permission to instruct a second paediatric neurologist in order to obtain a second opinion. Neither refusal was appealed to the Court of Appeal.

32.8   It was not until after the hearing on 8 April 2005 that the parents were successful in persuading a single member of the Court of Appeal that the papers should be released to a second expert. When that expert reported, his conclusion was fundamentally different to that of the first expert. In short, he took the view that the injuries had an innocent origin.

32.9   The consequence was that the orders made by the judge were, by consent, set aside by the Court of Appeal and the case was remitted to the High Court for re-hearing. On that re-hearing, the parents were vindicated. It was eventually agreed that the injuries suffered by the child had a natural cause. The result, however, was that the child had been separated from his parents for a year; that the parents had had to live with the finding of the court that they had abused their child when they had not done so, and the mother, who had become pregnant during the case, had undergone a termination of pregnancy rather than have the second child removed from her care at birth.

32.10   In the Court of Appeal, the court relied on and followed a decision in a non-family case called *Daniels v Walker*,[3] in which Lord Woolf, then the Master of the Rolls, had said:

> 27. Where a party sensibly agrees to a joint report and the report is obtained as a result of joint instructions in the manner which I have indicated, the fact that a party has agreed to adopt that course does not prevent that party being allowed facilities to obtain a report from another expert, or, if appropriate, to rely on the evidence of another expert.
>
> 28. In a substantial case such as this, the correct approach is to regard the instruction of an expert jointly as the first step in obtaining expert evidence on a particular issue. It is to be hoped that in the majority of cases it will not only be the first step but that the last step. If, having obtained a joint expert's report, a party, for reasons which are not fanciful, wishes to obtain further information before making a decision as to whether or not there is a particular part (or indeed the whole) of the expert's report which he or she may wish to challenge, then they should, subject to the discretion of the court, be permitted to obtain that evidence.[4]

32.11   At the conclusion of the re-hearing before Ryder J, everyone agreed (and the judge was at pains to point out) that the child had never been the victim of non-accidental injury, that his care by his parents had always been exemplary and that both his parents and relatives had acted promptly and appropriately in obtaining medical treatment for him.

32.12   The judge frankly acknowledged that this was a case in which a family court and an expert advising it had 'got it wrong' and that as a consequence there were lessons to be learned from the case.[5]

NOTES

1   Contrast *W v Oldham MBC* [2005] EWCA Civ 1247, [2007] EWHC 136 (Fam) (in which the opinion of the single, jointly instructed expert was found to be wrong and, if uncorrected, would have led to a serious miscarriage of justice, with *Re S; WSP v Hull City Council* [2006] EWCA Civ 981, in which the judge had been right to reject a call for further experts to be instructed.

2   Note 1 gives both the Court of Appeal reference and the reference to the subsequence judgment of Ryder J on the re-hearing. Although this chapter will set out some of what is said in both judgments, each repays study.

3   [2000] 1 WLR 1382, CA.

4   The Court of Appeal in *W v Oldham MBC* followed Lord Woolf's judgment on the basis of a submission made on behalf of the parents in the following terms:

> 'In many cases (probably the majority) a clear picture will emerge from a constellation of factors (eg paediatric, radiological, parental history, medical records) which will cumulatively point the court towards certain conclusions. Though those conclusions may be resisted by parents, it would be both unrealistic and unnecessary to permit parents to obtain "mirror reports" in every discipline. In a certain number of cases, however, eg non-accidental head injury (NAHI), or pathologically "unascertained" infant death, certain evidence may become pivotal and by its very nature not easily receptive to a challenge in the absence of any other expert opinion. In our submission, in those cases, the court should be slow to decline an application for a second expert. Strict case management (in accordance with the protocol) should also permit such evidence to be identified within a reasonable timescale.'

5   In his judgment at paragraph 91, Ryder J identified the following five points:

> In addition to the guidance formulated by the Court of Appeal in this case, I have also recommended that:
> (1)   Local authorities should always write a letter of instruction when asking a potential witness for a report or an opinion, whether that request is within proceedings or pre-proceedings eg when commissioning specialist assessment materials, reports from a treating expert or other evidential materials and the letter of instruction should conform to the principles set out by the Family Justice Council at www.family-justice-council.org.uk and the Chief Medical Officer at Annex B paragraph [21] of 'Bearing Good Witness' (2006) 30 October and Charles J in *A County Council v K, D and L* [2005] EWHC (Fam) 144, [2005] 1 FLR 851 paragraph 89;
> (2)   When requesting and collating existing materials, all parties should be vigilant to record requests of third parties for disclosure and their responses, so that the spectre of partial disclosure which tends only to prove a case rather than give full and frank information can be dispelled. Furthermore, great care must be exercised when placing reliance on materials that have not been produced either as 'original medical (or other professional) records' or in response to an instruction from a party as these materials may contain an assumption as to the standard of proof, the admissibility or otherwise of hearsay evidence and other important procedural and substantive questions that relate to the differing purposes of other enquiries (eg criminal or disciplinary proceedings);
> (3)   Once instructed, experts in their advice to the court should conform to the best practice of their clinical training and, in particular, should describe their own professional risk assessment process and/or the process of differential diagnosis that has been undertaken, highlighting factual assumptions, deductions there from and unusual features of the case. They should set out contradictory or inconsistent

features. They should identify the range of opinion on the question to be answered, giving reasons for the opinion they hold. They should highlight whether a proposition is a hypothesis (in particular a controversial hypothesis) or an opinion deduced in accordance with peer reviewed and tested technique, research and experience accepted as a consensus in the scientific community. They should highlight and analyse within the range of opinion an 'unknown cause', whether that be on the facts of the case (eg there is too little information to form a scientific opinion) or whether by reason of limited experience, lack of research, peer review or support in the field of skill and expertise that they profess. The use of a balance sheet approach to the factors that support or undermine an opinion can be of great assistance;

(4)   An expert should be asked at the earliest stage and in any event should volunteer an opinion whether another expert is required to bring a skill or expertise not possessed by those already involved or in the rare case a second opinion to a key issue that has been identified by the court and, if possible, what the question is that should be asked of that expert. In any event, far greater heed should be paid to advice from experts as to the questions that they are able to answer and that might be relevant to the court's determination;

(5)   The 'Code of Guidance for Expert Witnesses in Family Proceedings' at Appendix C to the Protocol (supra) should be amended to incorporate the recommendations made above.

(For the proposed alteration, see paragraph 3.2 in Appendix 11).

Chapter 33

WHAT IF YOU ARE THE TREATING CLINICIAN?

33.1 If you are a clinician involved in the clinical care of the patient, the likelihood is that you will not be asked to give an independent expert opinion in the case. It is much more likely that you will be asked to report on your clinical experience of the case, the factual events surrounding your involvement (for example interviews with parents on admission to A&E and subsequent discussions with them), your diagnosis and the treatment you administered or advised for the child. This does not mean, of course, that your evidence is not valuable to the court. The SHO who sees the child in A&E, describes the injuries and takes an early history from the parents is often a key witness in care proceedings. Equally, of course, clinicians charged with the patient's care may well themselves have consultant status.

33.2 In terms of the court's investigation and adjudication, however, lawyers tend to assign different roles to those involved with the care of the patient and those who advise the court as experts.[1]

33.3 A good example is a decision of the Court of Appeal in 2000.[2] The context was a treating psychiatrist expressing an opinion that a child had been sexually abused. The court in that case made it clear that the role of the treating expert was not to be muddled with that of the expert who was asked to provide an independent report for the court in proceedings relating to the child. A similar view was expressed in the report of Baroness Kennedy of the Shaws on Sudden Death in Infancy.[3]

33.4 There will, however, be occasions when clinical and expert responsibilities overlap. You may, for example, have a particular expertise which is engaged in the clinical diagnosis of a particular condition, about which you are subsequently asked to advise in an expert capacity. This duality of roles can cause problems for you.

33.5 In *W v Oldham MBC*[4] both the Court of Appeal and Ryder J addressed the point. The former[5] took the view that, whilst there was 'a clear distinction to be drawn between the functions of treating clinicians and expert witnesses', the fact that the doctor involved had had some clinical involvement by reason of his initial review of the relevant MRI scan, did not, of itself affect his capacity to act as an expert witness. The Court of Appeal accepted a submission made on behalf of the local authority that a blanket approach, which precluded treating clinicians from becoming jointly instructed witnesses in respect of children they have in fact treated, ran the risk of the court being deprived of expertise and excellence in those cases where children had been fortunate enough to have encountered clinically one of the diminishing number of doctors who are also ready willing and able to participate in the forensic process.[6]

33.6   In his judgment following the re-hearing, Ryder J commented that the court should not do anything to dissuade experts from providing the assistance that the court needs.[7]

33.7   If, therefore, you are a treating clinician who is asked to act as a jointly instructed expert witness, you should consider carefully whether or not you are in a position to provide the court with the objective information and opinion it requires from an independent expert. If in doubt, you should discuss the matter with the solicitor who is instructing you.

NOTES

1   An interesting recent example of the different functions of clinician and judge is provided by the case of *Re M-M (a child)* [2007] EWCA Civ 589. In that case a baby had a rare fracture of the ulna and a common place tibial fracture. The parents raised the possibility that the child suffered from osteogenesis imperfecta. The question for the judge was whether or not the injuries were non-accidental. The expert who was instructed to advise was of the opinion that osteogenesis imperfecta was 'extremely very unlikely', but then added:

> 'While the probability of a positive result here is very small, I believe it is advisable to carry out genetic testing as the level of proof must be as high as possible and having raised the possibility of testing in the cross-examination it would be wrong to dismiss testing on grounds of costs or inconvenience alone.'

The judge refused to authorise the test in the proceedings, and the parents appealed. Giving the leading judgment, Thorpe LJ said:

> 12.   … It does seem to me very important to draw a clear boundary between a medical decision as to what was clinically required in order to inform the future treatment of the child and a forensic decision as to what was necessary to ensure the proper determination of the issue in the causation hearing. Clearly the medical decision is for the doctors, and equally clearly the forensic decision is a case management decision for the judge.

> 13.   In the present case, the doctors were not expressing a medical opinion on clinical grounds and insofar as they ventured an opinion on what was forensically required, they were trespassing onto judicial territory. The discretion of the judge in taking case management decisions is particularly generous. The judge here clearly decided that enough was enough, and enough had been achieved in Professor P's considered view that in this particular child osteogenesis imperfecta was extremely unlikely. The judge clearly placed considerable emphasis on the fact that the expensive blood test which was urged upon her had been demonstrated to establish osteogenesis imperfecta in cases where there were no other clinical signs in only one percent of three hundred cases researched. The judge also attached weight to the fact that testing for osteogenesis imperfecta is only 90 percent accurate.

14. So this seems to me not only a permissible decision but a wise decision. There has to be a point at which the garnering of evidence is sufficiently full and thorough to enable the court to arrive at a conclusion, even on the elevated balance of probabilities standard of proof. It seems to me that Miss Wiley's argument comes close to saying that no stone must be left unturned. I do not accept that. The value to be derived from submitting this child to what is an invasive investigation was too small to justify the considerable cost both in cash and in time. I have no hesitation at all in upholding the judge's conclusion.

2   *Re B (Sexual Abuse: Expert's Report* [2000] 1 FLR 871. The treating psychiatrist had conducted an interview which immediately introduced anatomically correct dolls and included many leading questions. This was appropriate in the therapeutic context, but the questions were in plain breach of all the guidelines available to those conducting investigative interviews. The court said that the expert in question should not have accepted instructions to prepare a forensic report: she should have had the experience and the judgment to perceive that she was disqualified from making any forensic contribution by the nature of her medical reference and by the nature of the work which she had done in response to that reference.

3   The report of a working group convened by The Royal College of Pathologists and The Royal College of Paediatrics and Child Health, *The Role of the Expert Witness* published on 6 September 2004:

... It is our view that paediatricians involved in the acute management of patients should not be expected to give expert testimony in cases involving those patients. It is a sine qua non that doctors treating patients must develop partnerships with them and with the immediate family to ensure the best medical outcome. This will inevitably result in a degree of intimacy and therefore subjectivity when evaluating the case as a whole. This is the opposite of what is required of the expert witness, who should be objective, impartial and detached.

4   [2005] EWCA Civ 1247 and [2007] EWHC 136 (Fam): see Chapter 32 in which the facts of this case are set out.

5   [2005] EWCA Civ 1247 at paragraph 46.

6   The court added the rider, however, that: 'At the same time, ... the fact that an important opinion is being expressed by an expert who has had clinical involvement ... (provides) an additional argument for a second opinion, if one is called for by the parents.'

7   [2007] EWHC 136 at paragraph 98. He added that both forensic and treating experts will be subject to the same duties to the court and that treating experts of fact and opinion often provided the most valuable of original materials, including the immediate examination, recorded history and tests that may be difficult or impossible for a forensic expert to replicate. Such experts were and should be 'the first port of call for the local authority when it needs to commission specialist assessments and reports to inform its knowledge of the background and precipitating circumstances and its core assessment'.

Chapter 34

DIFFICULT MEDICAL ISSUES IN WHICH THE COURT HAS BECOME INVOLVED

34.1 As stated in Chapter 5, it is not the function of the court to become engaged in medical controversy, save in those exceptional cases in which the determination of medical issues is critical to outcome. One such area has been non-accidental head injuries (NAHI).

34.2 The general rule, of course, is that whilst judges have to decide the issues in a case, they cannot disagree with expert evidence without having good reasons for doing so and explaining why.[1] However, there are cases where the factual issue which the judge has to decide depends in whole or in part upon the judge's resolution of a disagreement between the medical experts on the causes of the condition from which the child in question is suffering.

34.3 There are, in particular, three reported cases which illustrate the point. In the first, a child of six months collapsed and died. His death could not be explained as SIDS or as arising from natural causes. There was, however, evidence that the child's eyes contained retinal haemorrhages but no evidence of cerebral haemorrhages. The majority expert opinion was that the retinal haemorrhages were sufficient to establish that, on the balance of probabilities, the death was non-accidental, resulting from an incident of shaking. The minority opinion was that the cause of death was unknown. The judge accepted the majority opinion.[2]

34.4 In the second case, the question was the degree of force required to produce acute subdural haematomas and bilateral retinal haemorrhages in a child aged five weeks.[3] The President of the Family Division, Dame Elizabeth Butler-Sloss, concluded that whilst there was medical controversy over the degree of force required to produce subdural haematomas, (and that the degree of force required was not as great as had previously been believed) it was nonetheless greater than that involved in the normal rough and tumble of family life. The parents had given an explanation for the injuries but their evidence was not accepted as credible and the judge concluded that the most probably cause was some form of shaking incident.[4]

34.5 The third case is a decision of the Court of Appeal.[5] The child in question was born prematurely and re-admitted to hospital approximately four weeks after being discharged. He was seriously ill and found to have subdural haemorrhages, although no other sign of injury. The two medical experts who gave evidence told the judge it was not possible to make a 'confident' diagnosis of non-accidental injury and that it was unusual to find non-accidental subdural haemorrhages of this type unaccompanied by any other physical injury. The judge found that the injuries were non-accidental and the Court of Appeal dismissed the parents' appeal against that finding.[6]

34.6   There have also been cases in which the judge has been required to investigate in detail the opinions of doctors who have written reports, which either set out to exonerate parents or which promulgated a particular theory – the clearest example being the so-called 'temporary brittle bone disease'. In such cases the judges have been severely critical of experts who have written misleading reports.

SUMMARY

34.7   The general rule is that judges only decide controversial medical issues when doing so is necessary for the resolution of the issues in the particular case.

NOTES

[1]   There are many cases in the books which support this proposition. See, for example, on BAILII *Re B (Non-accidental injury: compelling medical evidence)* [2002] EWCA Civ 902; *Re Y and K (Split Hearing: Evidence)* [2003] EWCA Civ 669; *A County Council v A Mother, A Father and X, Y and Z by their guardian* [2005] EWHC 31 (Fam); *A County Council v K, D and L* [2005] EWHC 144 (Fam).

[2]   *Re A (Non-Accidental Injury: Medical Evidence)* [2001] 2 FLR 657 (Bracewell J). The judge conducted a long and very careful analysis of the medical evidence, which repays study. At the outset she said:

> It is undoubtedly true that the frontiers of medical science are constantly being pushed back and that the state of knowledge is increasing all the time. That is why I find that when presented with a speculative theory based on an unlikely hypothetical base an expert will rarely discount it and will in effect never say never. Fanciful speculation is not an appropriate method of inquiry. What is needed and what the experts have done in this case is to piece together all the available information and look at the differential diagnosis. Many of the experts in this case specialise within a particular and very narrow field and by reason of being experts of referral at centres of excellence they acquire special knowledge and skill. However, concentration on a very narrow area of expertise can sometimes render it difficult for the expert to see the whole picture. In this regard I find that the pathologists are at a disadvantage when compared with the clinicians.

[3]   *Re A and D (Non-accidental injury: subdural haematomas)* [2002] 1 FLR 337.

[4]   The President, of course, decided the case on all the evidence, including her assessment of the parents' credibility. She was, however, specifically referred to the two papers by Geddes *et al* (including Professor Whitwell, from whom the judge heard oral evidence)

published in the medical journal (2001) 124 Brain 1290 et seq. The President added some general comments at the end of her judgment (paragraph 41):

> The Geddes et al research has posed questions in the related field of subdural haematomas but it has not provided answers. As I said earlier, further research on the mechanism of subdural haematomas and the degree of force required to cause them in young children and babies would be very helpful for the medical profession faced with the results of injury in hospital, for the child protection teams and for the judges and magistrates who try these cases. We must be careful not to jump to conclusions nor to accept too readily the diagnosis of non-accidental injury in these 'brain injury' cases. Equally there is no research that entitles us as judges to dismiss out of hand the clinical experience of paediatricians and other medical experts derived from examining in hospital these children and their injuries and investigating the circumstances in which the injuries were said to be caused. All the experts in this case came round to the opinion that the degree of force required to cause subdural haematomas need not be as great as previously believed. It remains however equally clear that the force used must be out of the normal rough and tumble of family life and must be unacceptable and inappropriate and obviously so. Each case of course has to be decided on its own facts. This is likely to be an evolving area of research. These are difficult cases: babies must be protected and parents or other carers must not be unfairly treated. The courts must however continue to deal with medical evidence on the basis of generally recognised medical opinion, giving due weight in the individual case to any advances in medical knowledge. This is a difficult area and in any case where contested issues on brain injury, subdural haematomas or retinal haemorrhages are raised in the immediate future, it would be wise for the court to consider where it would best be tried, depending upon the facts of the case and a realistic approach to the likely medical evidence to be called.

[5]   *Re B (Non-accidental injury)* [2002] EWCA Civ 752.

[6]   Giving the leading judgment, Thorpe LJ commented:

> It seems that ... the judge would have been failing in his primary protective function if he were to have acceded to some submission that because the doctor had not been prepared to say in medical language that there was a confident diagnosis therefore there was no evidence of risk of harm. The elevation of a medical opinion to the status of a confident medical diagnosis is very much a matter of art and bounded by medical conventions that are fully recognised and, indeed, negotiated at a professional level. What this doctor was saying was that the child's condition was entirely consistent with non-accidental injury and that there was no other more probable explanation. The case, in my view, is as straightforward as that. Although Mr Storey sought to say this is some dangerous invasion of the right of parents to presumptions of innocence and to safeguards from adverse findings absent the strongest and clearest of evidence, those submissions, in my opinion, are not realistic in the facts and circumstances of this particular case.

> The parents had their opportunity to make their contribution to the judicial investigation; they chose not to do so beyond submitting statements. It seems to me that although the judge, rightly, drew no inferences from that, there were inevitably risks of consequences for them in having stood aside.

Chapter 35

WILL YOU BE NAMED? ANONYMITY IN PROCEEDINGS RELATING TO CHILDREN

35.1 Family proceedings relating to children are currently heard in private and most judgments in cases involving children are also given in private. The reason for this is that Parliament, both in the Children Act 1989 and the Administration of Justice Act 1960, has made cases involving children an exception to the general rule that justice has to be done in public. The reason for Parliament's action is clear. It wanted to protect children from unnecessary and harmful publicity based on the behaviour of their parents over which, of course, they had no control.

35.2 Plainly, however, many cases decided in the family justice system are of considerable practical and public importance. Thus if judges at first instance decide cases which they think are of importance to the public or the legal or medical professions, the practice has been to publish the judge anonymously using initials only and concealing both the identities and whereabouts of the children concerned. This is why cases involving children are reported (often confusingly) under initials only.

35.3 Inevitably, the anonymity afforded to children has led to anonymity for their parents and other parties to care proceedings, including local authorities and experts. The result of this process, however, is that the family justice system has recently been accused of administering 'secret' justice. This in turn has led to an ongoing debate as to the extent to which the family justice system, consonant with protecting the privacy of children and families can properly open its doors to the media.

35.4 This Handbook is plainly not the place to continue the anonymity debate. However, the question does affect you in your capacity as expert witnesses. Are you content to be named in the court's judgment or should you remain anonymous?

35.5 At the moment, the question of anonymising a judgment is very much a matter for the individual judge. The practice is to anonymise, on the basis that identification of professionals (for example the name and location of the solicitors instructed in the case) could well facilitate identification of the children. On the other side, some attempts at anonymisation are patently transparent. If the leading expert on a particular illness is Professor Smith, it is no use calling the witness Professor S. Equally Professor M, in the context of factitious illness abuse, would not leave the intelligent reader guessing for very long.

35.6   My own practice at first instance varied. If I thought the public interest required the doctors in a case to be named, or if their identities were otherwise transparent, I would name them. The critical anonymity which the court seeks to protect, after all, is that of the child.

35.7   It would, however, be courteous if judges, when they have it in mind to identify in any subsequent judgment experts who have given evidence in front of them, were to alert the expert in question to the fact that he or she might be named. My personal view favours transparency, provided the identity and whereabouts of the children concerned is protected. From your perspective, being named is only likely to cause you professional harm if you have fallen below the standard demanded by your profession and are properly criticised by the judge. If, as this Handbook constantly states, you have done your work conscientiously you have nothing to fear from the courts.

35.8   It is, perhaps, worth pointing out that in the Court of Appeal, every word spoken in every child case is spoken in public and is capable of being reported, subject of course to the rule that, in appropriate cases, the children concerned should not be identified. My personal view is that greater openness will show the public the extreme difficulty and sensitivity of the decisions judges have to make, and how conscientiously they go about making them. I see no reason why you should not share fully in that process.

Chapter 36

THE BRITISH AND IRISH
LEGAL INFORMATION INSTITUTE (BAILII)

36.1   It may seem odd, in a Handbook which, on the whole, seeks to limit the number of references to cases decided in the courts, to contain a chapter describing a particular legal search engine. The reason for doing so, however, will, I hope, rapidly become apparent.

36.2   Doctors and lawyers do not, as a general rule, read each others' journals. Most of us have enough difficulty keeping up to date in our own particular field of activity and, unless something is required reading for the case in hand, we simply do not have either the time or the inclination to keep abreast of what is happening in a different discipline.[1] For the lawyer, articles in medical journals are often very technical and thus difficult for the lay person to understand. No doubt you feel the same about articles in legal journals.

36.3   You are, of course, an expert witness, not a lawyer. There will, however, be times when a particular judgment of the court raises important medical issues and others when it will be important for you to know what is going on at the medical/legal interface. The decision of the Court of Appeal in *Meadow v GMC* is one example. *R (Burke) v GMC*[2] is another. You are unlikely to have ready access to the Law Reports or to have a subscription to any on-line legal data base. You are, of course, entitled to feedback on the attitude to your report taken by the court in any case in which you are involved,[3] and you can always ask the solicitor instructing you (or the lead solicitor if you are jointly instructed) to bring you up to speed on any legal issues relevant to the instructions you have received in the case in which you are writing your report. But, sometimes, there will be no substitute for familiarising yourself with a particular decision by a judge, the Court of Appeal or the House of Lords.

36.4   One of the most helpful developments since the first edition of this work has been the creation of BAILII. The letters stand for the British and Irish Legal Information Institute. BAILII provides free access via the internet to what it legitimately describes as 'the most comprehensive set of British and Irish primary legal materials that are available for free and in one place on the internet'.

36.5   BAILII's address on the internet is http://www.bailii.org. The website also provides its mailing and email addresses, as well as telephone numbers, although it does not generally provide any services via these routes. The database contains all the important decisions of the House of Lords and the Court of Appeal, as well as those decisions of judges of the Family Division which have been given in open court and which the judge has arranged to be reported on BAILII.[4]

36.6   Each reported case is given what is called a 'neutral citation number'. The code is self-explanatory, and comprises the year in which the case was decided (in square brackets) followed by the identity of the tribunal and a number. Thus the decision of the Civil Division of the Court of Appeal for England and Wales in *Meadow v GMC* has the neutral citation number [2006] EWCA Civ 1390: the decision of the High Court Judge (Collins J) at first instance in the Administrative Court has the neutral citation number [2006] EWHC 146 (Admin). The decision of Criminal Division of the Court of Appeal in the case of Angela Cannings (entitled *R v Cannings*) has the neutral citation number [2004] EWCA Crim 01; the judgment of the Criminal Division of the Court of Appeal quashing Sally Clark's conviction (*R v Clark*) is [2003] EWCA Crim 1020. *R (Burke) v GMC* has the neutral citation number [2005] EWCA Civ 1003. Decisions of judges in the Family Division of the High Court have the suffix EWHC (Fam).

36.7   Decisions of the House of Lords,[5] of course, cover the whole of the United Kingdom. The neutral citation numbers of these decisions are, accordingly, the year in brackets followed by UKHL and the number.

36.8   The policy of this Handbook remains not to refer to decided cases unless it is strictly necessary. However, when a specific case is mentioned, its neutral citation number (if it has one) will be given. This should enable you to find the case on BAILII if you wish to read it. Moreover, as explained in the Note on Cases Referred to in the Handbook on page xvii, the publishers have helpfully agreed with BAILII a simple method whereby you can gain easy access to any judgment referred to in this Handbook.

36.9   As paragraph **36.4** above makes clear, a major benefit of BAILII is that it is free. It also contains a search facility, if you do not know either the name of the case you are looking for, or its neutral citation number.

36.10   The number of judgments by judges of the Family Division at first instance is, currently, limited to those in which the judge has (1) reserved judgment, (2) delivered or handed it down in open court; and / or given permission for it to be reported and (3) arranged for it to be reported on BAILII.[6]

36.11   There are currently very few judgments of judges of the High Court of the Family Division on BAILII. It is to be hoped that judges will, increasingly, give their judgments in open court so that both you and the public at large will have a much better appreciation of the thought and care which goes into making what are often very difficult decisions. Such a process will also enable you to see how the judge has addressed your evidence in any case in which you have been involved.

36.12   You will, of course, have your own methods of using the internet. If you go to the BAILII website, however, you will be offered immediate access to the England and Wales database which, in turn, will give you access to all of the courts whose decisions feature in this Handbook. Alternatively, all the cases cited herein can be easily accessed from a single page at the following address: http://www.bailii.org/books/experts_handbook.html.

NOTES

[1]   If you have the time to look at it, the nearest approximation to an interdisciplinary journal is *Family Law* published monthly by Jordans Publishing. It covers what is happening throughout the Family Justice System, and apart from identifying important cases, regularly has articles dealing with the medical / legal interface.

[2]   See paragraph **36.6** below.

[3]   See Chapter 26 and paragraph 7.1 of Appendix C to the Public Law Protocol set out in that chapter.

[4]   There is an increasing trend towards transparency in family justice, which includes judgments being given in open court.

[5]   Renamed the Supreme Court by section 23 of the Constitutional Reform Act 2005, decisions of the House of Lords can also be accessed via the House of Lords judicial website: http://www.publications.parliament.uk/pa/ld/ldjudgmt.htm.

[6]   Family judges sitting in the High Court are being encouraged to put their reserved decisions on BAILII.

Appendix 1

SUGGESTED FURTHER READING

1   *Handbook of Best Practice in Children Act Cases* Children Act Advisory
    Committee (DOH, June 1997).
2   *The Expert Witness Pack for use in Children Proceedings* (see the
    attached CD-ROM).
3   Williams C 'Expert Evidence in Cases of Child Abuse' *Archives of Disease
    in Childhood* 1993; 68: 712–14.
4   Wall N Judicial Attitudes to Expert Evidence in Children's Cases. *Archives
    of Disease in Childhood* 1997; 76: 485–89.
5   David TJ, Hershman DA, McFarlane AE: Pre-trial Liaison between
    Doctors in Alleged Child Abuse: *Archives of Disease in Childhood* 1998;
    79: 205–6.
6   Cottrell and Tufnell 'Expert Reports: What Constitutes Good Practice'
    [1996] Fam Law 159 and Tufnell 'Psychiatric Court Reports in Child Care
    Cases: What Constitutes "Good Practice"?' (1993) 15 *Association of Child
    Psychology and Psychiatry Review and Newsletter* pp 219–24.
7   Wall N (ed) *Rooted Sorrows: Psychoanalytic Perspectives on Child
    Protection, Assessment, Therapy and Treatment* (Family Law, 1997).
8   Thorpe M and Clarke E (eds) *Divided Duties – Care Planning for
    Children within the Family Justice System* (Family Law, 1998).
9   Walsh, Elizabeth *Working in the Family Justice System, A Guide for
    Professionals* (2nd edn, Family Law, 2006).
10 Black, Harris-Hendriks and Wolkind (eds) *Child Psychiatry and the Law*
    (3rd edn, Gaskell, 1998).
11 Carty, H 'Doctor at Law' [1999] Fam Law 391.
12 Plotnikoff and Woolfson *Reporting to Court under the Children Act (A
    Handbook for Social Services)* (DOH, 1996).
13 Pamplin C *Expert Witness Fees*, J S Publications (Newmarket, 2007).
14 Golan T *Laws of Men and Laws of Nature. The History of Scientific
    Expert Testimony in England and America* (Harvard University Press,
    2004).

Appendix 2

THE FAMILY JUSTICE COUNCIL

TERMS OF REFERENCE

The terms of reference of the FJC specifically includes:

1 The promotion of improved interdisciplinary working across the family justice system through inclusive discussion, communication and co-ordination between all agencies, including by way of seminars and conferences as appropriate;
2 The identification and dissemination of best practice throughout the family justice system by facilitating a mutual exchange of information between local FJCs and the national Council, including information on local initiatives, and by identifying priorities for, and encouraging the conduct of, research;
3 The provision of guidance and direction to achieve consistency of practice throughout the family justice system and submit proposals for new practice directions where appropriate;
4 The provision of advice and recommendations to Government on changes to legislation, practice and procedure, which will improve the workings of the family justice system.

MEMBERSHIP OF THE EXPERTS SUB-COMMITTEE OF THE FJC

Appointed FJC members of the Experts committee

Chair	Rt Honourable Lord Justice Thorpe, Deputy Head of Family Justice
Barrister	Stephen Cobb QC
Solicitor (public law)	Katherine Gieve
Solicitor (private law)	Jane Craig
Child mental health specialist	Danya Glaser
Paediatrician	Rosalyn Proops

Co-opted members of the Experts committee [as at May 2007]

General Medical Council	Dr Joan Trowell (also lecturer in medicine and a consultant physician)
Forensic Psychology	Professor Jane Ireland
Clinical Psychology	Professor Ray Bull / John Pinschoff
Child Psychiatry	Dr Mike Shaw / Dr Greg Richardson
Paediatrics (Education & Training)	Dr Christopher Verity
Radiology	Dr Karl Johnson
Ophthalmology	Dr Michael Clarke
Neuro-radiology	Dr Neil Stoodley
Neurology	Dr Colin Ferrie
CAFCASS	Christine Smart
Ministry of Justice	Jodie Smith

Proposed model questions in letters of instruction to child mental health professionals or paediatricians in Children Act 1989 proceedings

A. *The Child(ren)*

1. Please describe the child(ren)'s current health, development and functioning (according to your area of expertise), and identify the nature of any significant changes which have occurred
    Behavioural
    Emotional
    Attachment organisation
    Social / peer / sibling relationships
    Cognitive / educational
    Physical
        Growth, eating, sleep
        Non-organic physical problems (including wetting and soiling)
        Injuries
        Paediatric conditions.
2. Please comment on the likely explanation for / aetiology of the child(ren)'s problems / difficulties / injuries
    History / experiences (including intrauterine influences, and abuse and neglect)

Genetic / innate / developmental difficulties

Paediatric / psychiatric disorders.

3. Please provide a prognosis and risk if difficulties above are not addressed.

4. Please describe the child(ren)'s needs in the light of the above

Nature of care-giving

Education

Treatment

in the short and long term (subject, where appropriate, to further assessment).

B. The parents/primary care-givers

5. Please describe the factors and mechanisms which would explain the parents' (or primary care-givers') harmful or neglectful interactions with the child(ren) (if relevant).

6. What interventions have been tried and what has been the result?

7. Please assess the ability of the parents or primary care-givers to fulfil the child(ren)'s identified needs now.

8. What other assessments of the parents or primary care-givers are indicated

Adult mental health assessment

Forensic risk assessment

Physical assessment

Cognitive assessment.

9. What, if anything, is needed to assist the parents or primary care-givers now, within the child(ren)'s time scales and what is the prognosis for change

Parenting work

Support

Treatment / therapy.

C. Alternatives

10. Please consider the alternative possibilities for the fulfilment of the child(ren)'s needs.

What sort of placement

Contact arrangements

Please consider the advantages, disadvantages and implications of each for the child(ren).

PROPOSED MODEL QUESTIONS IN LETTERS OF INSTRUCTION TO ADULT PSYCHIATRISTS IN CHILDREN ACT 1989 PROCEEDINGS

1 Does the parent / adult have a mental illness / disorder (including substance abuse) and if so, what is the diagnosis?

2   Does the parent's / adult's history or presentation indicate any features of personality disorder?

3   How do either / both of the above (and their current treatment if applicable) affect his / her functioning, including interpersonal relationships?

4   If the answer to Q 1 or 2 is yes, are there any features of either the mental illness or personality disorder which could be associated with risk to others, based on the available evidence base?

5   What are the experiences / antecedents / aetiology which would explain his / her difficulties, if any?

6   What treatment is indicated, what is its nature and the likely duration?

7   What is his / her capacity to engage in / partake of the treatment / therapy?

8   Are you able to indicate the prognosis for, time scales for achieving, and likely durability, of change?

9   What other factors might indicate positive change?

(It is assumed that this opinion will be based on collateral information as well as interviewing the adult.)

Appendix 3

CARE CENTRES AND THEIR DESIGNATED FAMILY JUDGES

BIRMINGHAM

His Honour Judge D Hamilton
Birmingham Civil Trial Centre
Priory Courts
33 Bull Street
Birmingham B4 6DS

BLACKBURN

Her Honour Judge B Watson
Blackburn County Court
64 Victoria Street
Blackburn BB1 6DJ

BOURNEMOUTH

His Honour Judge R Bond
Bournemouth Crown and County Court
Courts of Justice
Deansleigh Road
Bournemouth BH7 7DS

BRIGHTON

His Honour Judge S Lloyd
Brighton County Court
Family Hearing Centre
1 Edward Street
Brighton BN2 0JD

BRISTOL

Her Honour Judge S Darwall-Smith
Bristol County Court
Greyfriars
Lewins Mead
Bristol BS1 2NR

CAENARVON

His Honour Judge M Farmer QC
Caenarvon County Court
The Court House
Llanberis Road
Caenarvon LL55 2DF

CAMBRIDGE

Her Honour Judge I Plumstead
Cambridge Court Court
197 East Road
Cambridge CB1 1BA

CANTERBURY

His Honour Judge D Cryan
Canterbury Combined Court Centre
The Law Courts
Chancer Road
Canterbury CT1 1ZA

CARDIFF

His Honour Judge C Masterman
Cardiff Civil Justice Centre
2 Park Street
Cardiff CF10 1ET

CARLISLE

Her Honour Judge B Forrester
Carlisle Combined Court Centre
Courts of Justice
East Street
Carlisle CA1 1DJ

CHELMSFORD

His Honour Judge G Gypps
Chelmsford County Court
London Road
New London Road
Chelmsford CM2 0QR

CHESTER

His Honour Judge K Barnett
Chester Civil Justice Centre
Trident House
Little St John Street
Chester CH1 1SN

COVENTRY

His Honour Judge C Bellamy
Coventry Combined Court Centre
140 Much Park Street
Coventry CV1 2SN

DERBY

His Honour Judge J Orrell
Derby Combined Court Centre
Morledge
Derby DE1 2XE

EXETER

His Honour Judge D Tyzack QC
Exeter Combined Court Centre
Southernhay Gardens
Exeter EX1 1UH

GUILDFORD

His Honour Judge S Sleeman
Guildford County Court
The Law Courts
Mary Road
Guildford GU1 4PS

IPSWICH

Her Honour Judge C Ludlow
Ipswich County Court
8 Arcade Street
Ipswich IP1 1EJ

HUMBERSIDE

Mr Justice J Dowse
Kingston upon Hull Combined Court Centre
Lowgate
Humberside HU1 2EZ

LEEDS

Her Honour Judge P Hunt
Leeds Civil Hearing Centre
The Court House
1 Oxford Row
Leeds LS1 3BG

LEICESTER

His Honour Judge D Brunning
Leicester County Court
90 Wellington Street
Leicester LE1 6JG

LINCOLN

His Honour Judge R Jenkins
Lincoln Combined Court Centre
360 High Street
Lincoln LN5 7PS

LIVERPOOL

Her Honour Judge M de Haas QC
Liverpool Civil and Family Court
35 Vernon Street
Liverpool L2 2BX

LONDON

His Honour Judge J Altman
Royal Courts of Justice
Strand
London WC2A 2LL

LUTON

His Honour Judge J Farnworth
Luton County Court
2nd Floor, Cresta House
Alma Street
Luton LU1 2PU

MANCHESTER

His Honour Judge I Hamilton
Manchester County Court
The Court House
184–186 Deansgate
Manchester M3 3WB

MIDDLESBROUGH

His Honour Judge D Bryant
Teeside Combined Court Centre
Russell Street
Middlesbrough TS1 2AE

NEWCASTLE

Her Honour Judge J Moir
Newcastle upon Tyne Combined Court Centre
The Law Courts
The Quayside
Newcastle-upon-Tyne
Tyne & Wear NE1 3LA

NEWPORT

His Honour Judge M Furness
Newport County Court
Olympia House
3rd Floor Upper Dock Street
Newport
Gwent NP20 1PQ

NORTHAMPTON

His Honour Judge S Waine
Northampton Combined Court
85/87 Lady's Lane
Northampton NN1 3HQ

NORWICH

His Honour Judge Curl
Norwich Combined Court Centre
The Law Courts
Bishopsgate
Norwich NR3 1UR

NOTTINGHAM

Her Honour Judge J Butler QC
Nottingham County Court
60 Canal Street
Nottingham NG1 7EJ

PORTSMOUTH

Her Honour Judge L Davies
Portsmouth Combined Court Centre
The Courts of Justice
Winston Church Avenue
Portsmouth PO1 2EB

READING

His Honour Judge C Elly
Reading County Court
160–163 Friar Street
Reading RG1 1HE

RHYL

His Honour Judge M Farmer QC
Rhyl County Court
The Court House
Clwyd Street
Rhyl LL18 3LA

SHEFFIELD

His Honour Judge T Barber
Sheffield Combined Court Centre
The Law Courts
50 West Bar
Sheffield S3 8PH

STOKE ON TRENT

His Honour Judge G Styler
Stoke on Trent Combined Court Centre
Bethesda Street
Hanley
Stoke on Trent ST1 3BP

SWANSEA

Her Honour Judge I Parry
Swansea County Court
Carvella House
Quay West, Quay Street
Swansea SA1 4PF

SWINDON

His Honour Judge J McNaught
Swindon County Combined Court
The Law Courts
Islington Street
Swindon SN1 2HG

TAUNTON

His Honour Judge S O'Malley
Taunton County Court
The Shire Hall
Taunton TA1 4EU

TRURO

His Honour Judge N Vincent
Truro County Court
Courts of Justice
Edward Street
Truro
Cornwall TR1 2PB

WOLVERHAMPTON

Her Honour Judge H Hughes
Wolverhampton Combined Court Centre
Pipers Row
Wolverhampton WV1 3LQ

WATFORD

His Honour Judge J Mitchell
Watford County Court
Cassiobury House
11–19 Station Road
Watford
Hertfordshire WD17 1EZ

WORCESTER

His Honour Judge R Rundell
Worcester Combined Court Centre
The Shorehall
Foregate Street
Worcester WR1 1EQ

YORK

His Honour Judge G Cliffe
York County Court
Piccadilly House
55 Piccadilly
York YO1 9WL

Appendix 4

HER MAJESTY'S COURTS SERVICE ESTATE BY REGION AND AREA AND THE FAMILY DIVISION LIAISON JUDGES

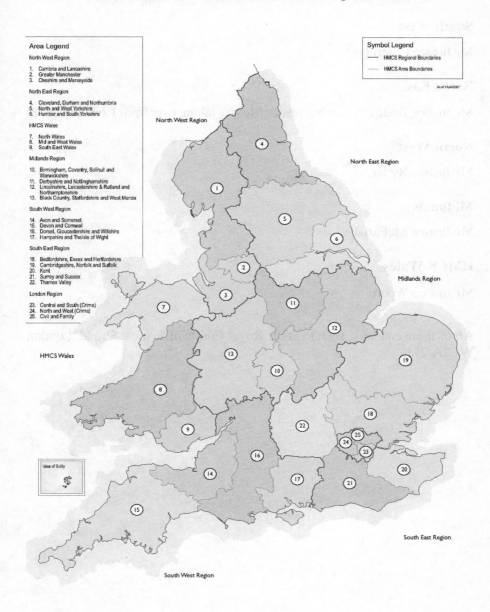

Area Legend

North West Region

1. Cumbria and Lancashire
2. Greater Manchester
3. Cheshire and Merseyside

North East Region

4. Cleveland, Durham and Northumbria
5. North and West Yorkshire
6. Humber and South Yorkshire

HMCS Wales

7. North Wales
8. Mid and West Wales
9. South East Wales

Midlands Region

10. Birmingham, Coventry, Solihull and Warwickshire
11. Derbyshire and Nottinghamshire
12. Lincolnshire, Leicestershire & Rutland and Northamptonshire
13. Black Country, Staffordshire and West Mercia

South West Region

14. Avon and Somerset
15. Devon and Cornwall
16. Dorset, Gloucestershire and Wiltshire
17. Hampshire and The Isle of Wight

South East Region

18. Bedfordshire, Essex and Hertfordshire
19. Cambridgeshire, Norfolk and Suffolk
20. Kent
21. Surrey and Sussex
22. Thames Valley

London Region

23. Central and South (Crime)
24. North and West (Crime)
25. Civil and Family

Symbol Legend

— HMCS Regional Boundaries
— HMCS Area Boundaries

As at 1 April 2007

THE FAMILY DIVISION LIAISON JUDGES

South East

Mrs Justice Macur   (Mrs Justice Baron taking over from 1 January 2008)

Mrs Justice Pauffley

Mr Justice Hedley (London)

South West

Mr Justice Coleridge

North East

Mr Justice Bodey   (Mr Justice Moylan taking over from 1 January 2008)

North West

Mr Justice Ryder

Midlands

Mr Justice McFarlane

HMCS Wales

Mr Justice Wood

All of these can be written to at the Royal Courts of Justice, Strand, London WC2A 2LL.

Appendix 5

A NOTE ON JUDICIAL TITLES
AND LAW REPORTS

1   Judicial titles are complicated and not always consistent. Fortunately, all you really need to know is how to address the judge in court – see Chapter 23. Equally, if you meet a judge of either gender off the bench (for example, at a conference) you cannot go wrong if you address either him or her as 'judge'. 'Dear Judge' is also the correct way to address a judge if you have to write to one. This applies even if the judge concerned is a member of the Court of Appeal, although, technically, such a judge should be addressed as either 'Lord Justice' or 'Lady Justice'. So far, so good.

THE SUPREME COURT (AKA THE HOUSE OF LORDS)

2   The technical term for the House of Lords sitting in its judicial capacity was the Judicial Committee of the House of Lords. The 11 judges appointed to sit in the House of Lords all remain Peers of the Realm, despite the fact that they currently sit in what has been renamed the Supreme Court. Since they have all been appointed from the Court of Appeal, are all members of the Privy Council. The one woman is Baroness Hale of Richmond: the others are all Lords. Their official titles, accordingly, are the Rt Hon Lord X.

THE COURT OF APPEAL

3   There are 39 members of the Court of Appeal. They are called Lords / Lady Justices of Appeal. The shorthand is LJ (singular) and LJJ (plural). In both cases, for some reason, the abbreviation follows the surname (ie Smith LJ or Smith and Jones LJJ).

4   Members of the Court of Appeal are appointed to the Privy Council, so they are Right Honourable. The correct way to write to a member of the Court of Appeal is thus 'The Rt Hon Lord / Lady Justice Smith'. If you are feeling particularly energetic, you can begin your letter 'Dear Lord / Lady Justice Smith' but, frankly, 'judge' does just as well.

5   The most senior judge and head of the judiciary is the Lord Chief Justice. In the Family Jurisdiction, the most senior judge is the President of the Family

Division, currently Sir Mark Potter. He is referred to in Law Reports as Sir Mark Potter P. The President of the Family Division does not have the title of Lord Justice, although he is a senior member of the Court of Appeal and ranks fourth in seniority after the Lord Chief Justice, the Master of the Rolls (who heads the Civil Division of Court of Appeal) and the Chancellor, who heads the Chancery Division of the High Court. The President sits both at first instance on his own as a Judge of the High Court and also in the Court of Appeal, where he presides, unless sitting with a judge who is senior to him such as the Lord Chief Justice.

6   The President is thus addressed in correspondence as 'the Rt Hon Sir Mark Potter' and any letter to him should begin 'Dear President'. You should also address him as 'President' if you meet him socially. In court, of course, he is addressed as 'My Lord'. The Family jurisdiction also has a Deputy Head of Family Justice and Head of International Family Justice, who is currently Thorpe LJ.

THE HIGH COURT

7   For the remaining judicial titles described all the judges identified will be called Smith. There are 110 High Court judges, of whom 19 are assigned to the Family Division of the High Court. Male High Court judges are knighted and female High Court judges are appointed DBE. It is therefore an anomaly that their official titles are Mr Justice Smith and Mrs Justice Smith. The correct way to write to a High Court judge is to address him or her as 'The Honourable (Hon) Mr / Mrs Justice Smith'. But you still begin the letter, 'Dear Judge'. In court you call a High Court Judge 'My Lord' or 'My Lady' according to gender.

8   When High Court judges retire, they lose the 'Hon' but retain the knighthood / DBE. For some reason I don't understand, female High Court Judges are usually written to as 'The Hon Mrs Justice Smith DBE', whereas male High Court judges should be written to as 'the Hon Mr Justice Smith'.

9   High Court judges are designated in the Law Reports by the letter J (short for Mr / Mrs Justice) after their surname. Thus Mr Justice Smith will appear as Smith J, and Mr Justice Smith and Mrs Justice Jones will appear as Smith and Jones JJ.

THE CIRCUIT BENCH AND RECORDERS

10   Circuit judges and recorders are addressed in court as 'Your Honour'. Their correct title if you have to write to a circuit judge is 'His / Her Honour Judge Smith'. If Judge Smith was a QC at the bar, he or she will tend, quite illogically, to retain the title so as to be 'His / Her Honour Judge Smith QC'. A retired circuit judge loses the 'judge' if you write to him or her,

thus 'His Honour John / Jane Smith'. You can, however, still write to them as 'judge' and so address them when you meet. Nobody seems to mind being called 'judge'.

11 Recorders are usually practising members of the legal profession but will be flattered if you write to them or address them as 'judge'. The correct mode of address in correspondence is 'Dear Recorder Smith' or 'Dear Recorder Smith QC' if Recorder Smith is a QC.

DISTRICT JUDGES AND LAY JUSTICES

12 There are two kinds of district judge. There is the district judge who sits in the Magistrates' Court, usually hearing only criminal cases. The principal exception is the Inner London Family Proceedings Court where the District Judge, Nicholas Crichton, sits exclusively in family cases. This type of district judge used to be called a Stipendiary Magistrate (ie paid) in order to distinguish them from lay magistrates, who are not paid. Their abbreviated title is DJ(MC). In court you would address a DJ(MC) as 'sir' or 'madam' according to gender. You would write to them as District Judge X, and the letter can begin 'Dear District Judge' or even 'Dear Judge' (they won't mind).

13 More relevant for your purposes, however, are district judges who sit in the county court. They are a tier below the Circuit Judges, although in family cases a large number of district judges are ticketed[1] (that is to say authorised by the President and given extra training by the Judicial Studies Board) to sit to hear contested applications, both in private and public law, and exercise the same jurisdiction as the circuit bench (see also Appendix 9). When sitting in this latter capacity they are addressed as 'Your Honour'. Otherwise, they are 'Sir' or 'Madam' according to gender. If you have to give evidence before a DJ (the customary abbreviation) and you are unsure how to address him or her, ask counsel to tell you.

14 Lay magistrates (Justices of the Peace or JPs) also sit to hear family cases, and can exercise the same jurisdiction as the county court and the High Court. If you appear in front of a lay bench, you address your evidence to the chair, whom you call either 'Sir' or 'Madam' according to gender.

15 I hope this gives you some idea. Don't worry about it. I do not imagine you will often have to write to the Lord Chief Justice or the President of the Family Division. If you do, and you remain concerned, either cite this book or get your secretary to telephone theirs to find out how to address them!

LAW REPORTS

16 As you might expect, there are a number of different law reports in which family cases can be found. What follows is a rough survey. I will also, for

ease of reference, identify one case which appears in all the different reports.

17   The advantage of law reports, when you have access to them, is that they all have headnotes which, as pointed out footnote 2 to paragraph 1.4 of this Handbook, enables the reader to identify both the point of the case and the relevant parts of the judgment. Summaries (in the various journals set out below) are also very helpful.

18   The Official Law reports are published by The Incorporated Council of Law Reporting (ICLR) of Megarry House, 119 Chancery Lane, London, WC2A 1PP. These cover the House of Lords, the Court of Appeal and the various Divisions of the High Court. They are the only law reports which, in appropriate cases, report the arguments advanced by counsel as well as the approved text of the court's judgment. The family cases in this series are designed by the year in square brackets followed by the word 'Fam' and the page number. Thus the important decision of the Court of Appeal relating to domestic violence and contact (for which the report by Drs Glaser and Sturge was written) appears as *In Re L (A Child) (Contact: Domestic Violence) In Re V (A Child) In Re M (A Child) In Re H (Children)* [2001] Fam 260.

19   The ICLR also publish the Weekly Law Reports which, as their name suggests, are published in weekly instalments over the year, but do not at that stage include the arguments of counsel. The parts are then bound up into three volumes. Volume 1 contains reports not destined for the official Law Reports. These do not include the arguments of counsel: Volumes 2 and 3 comprise cases which are then usually reproduced, with the arguments of counsel, in the official Law Reports. Cases are designated by the year in square brackets followed by the volume and page numbers. Thus, the designation of *Re L* in the Weekly Law Reports was [2001] 2 WLR 339. Such has been the increase in the volume of cases reported that in recent years, volume one of the WLR has had itself to be divided up into two thick bound volumes, designated (in 2006) as [2006] 1 WLR Part 1 and [2006] 1 WLR Part 2.

20   There are two principal series of specialist law reports. These are the Family Law Reports (FLR) published by Jordans, and the Family Court Reports (FCR) published by Butterworths. The latter appear fortnightly: the former periodically during the course of the year. The FLR are then bound up into two volumes, and the FCR bound up into three. Thus *Re L* appeared in the Family Law Reports as [2000] 2 FLR 334, and in the Family Court Reporter as [2000] 2 FCR 404.

21   Jordans also publish the monthly Family Law journal (Fam Law), to which a reference is made in the footnote to paragraph **36.2** of the text of this Handbook. Fam Law publishes monthly digests of important cases, and a summary of *Re L*, with a commentary by Professor Rebecca Bailey-Harris, appears under the designation (2000) Fam Law 603.

22 Family law cases do not often appear in the other major series of law reports, namely the All England Law Reports (All ER) which appear weekly, and are also published by Butterworths. These are bound up annually into four volumes. However, family cases which are deemed to be of wider interest do appear in the All England Law Reports, and *Re L* is reported in this series at [2000] 4 All ER 609. Butterworth also operates a service which summarises important cases, and *Re L* here appears as [2000] All ER (D) 827, CA.

23 Summaries of important cases are also contained in the Solicitors Journal, a legal periodical, and *Re L* appears here in volume 144 under the designation 144 Sol. Jo. LB 222.

24 These are a number of other journals and specialist publications which provide useful information speedily, both on paper and electronically. Those set out above, however can, I think, fairly be called the major sources.

25 Unlike BAILII (see Chapter 36) all of the above have to be paid for.

---

[1] 'Ticketed' is rather a loose term. It can apply to different judges in different spheres, both civil and criminal, and is part of a system designed to ensure that a judge has the particular expertise required to hear a particular case. Thus some criminal judges have what is loosely called 'a serious sex ticket'. Family Circuit judges are given 'public law' or 'care tickets' by the President of the Family Division to enable them, after appropriate training, to hear care cases. Most recorders and county court district judges only have a private law ticket, and can thus only hear private law cases.

Appendix 6

SUGGESTED STANDARD DOCUMENT IN RELATION TO FEES / CHARGES

Name

Post currently held / status / area of expertise

Address

Scale of charges for medico-legal work 2007

Preparation

Perusing documents/preparation	£ xxxx per hour
Undertaking examination/interviews	£ xxx per hour

Writing report   £ xxx per hour

Telephone calls / correspondence	£ xxx per item

(if charged separately – practice varies)

Attendances

Attending meetings	£ xxx per hour

Attending Court

Half day	£ xxx
Whole day	£ xxx

Travelling

Travel to Court / meetings	£ xxx per hour plus expenses

Appendix 7

MODEL FEE NOTE

Name & address of
instructing solicitors

Case name & court number

To professional fees relating to [describe broad remit of work i.e. undertaking
and reporting on paediatric assessment of …, or reviewing medical records
and x-rays and providing a report on … or undertaking psychiatric/psychological
assessment of and a report on …] to include

Preparation

Date	Perusal & consideration of documents	2.5 hours @ £x	£xxx
Date	Perusal & consideration of further documents preparatory to attending meeting of experts	1.5 hours @ £x	£xxx
Date	Reviewing documents & preparing to attend to give evidence	3.0 hours @ £x	£xxx

Examination/Attendances

Date	Medical/psychiatric/psychological examination of patient/subject	1.5 hours @ £x	£xxx
Date	Further examination of subject	1.0 hour @ £x	£xxx
Date	Attending Meeting of Experts	2.25 hours @ £x	£xxx
Date	Attending conference with counsel/advocate	1.5 hours @ £x	£xxx

Court Attendance

Date	Conferring with advocates/ other experts	1.25 hours @ £x	£xxx
	Waiting	2.0 hours @ £x	£xxx
	Hearing	2.0 hours @ £x	£xxx

Travelling

Date	Meeting of Medical Experts	2.5 hours @ £x	£xxx
	Conference with counsel	2.0 hours @ £x	£xxx
	Anytown County Court	2.5 hours @ £x	£xxx

Telephone calls/correspondence

Date(s)	Itemise those for which charge to be made	7 @ £x	£xxx

Expenses

Date	Travel [itemise details] x miles @ x pence per mile	£xxx
Date	Parking	£xxx
	Total	**£xxx**

Appendix 8

EXPERT WITNESS TERMS OF ENGAGEMENT IN LEGALLY AIDED CHILDREN ACT PROCEEDINGS

[*Name of Firm*] holds a Legal Services Commission Franchise Contract in Family Law. This imposes obligations and requirement which the practice must fulfil in relation to the provision of services to clients who are funded by the Community Legal Service. Experts instructed by [*Name of Firm*] have to be identified as being able to provide a standard and quality of service which enable us to be able to meet our franchise obligations. Experts who fail to meet those standards cannot remain or be placed on the list of 'Approved Experts' which the practice is required to maintain and review on a continuing basis.

Solicitors undertaking Community Legal Service Fund work have a duty to the Legal Services Commission, and their clients, to ensure that costs and fees incurred in the conduct of any cases are reasonably necessary. Under the Funding Code, Solicitors are only permitted to pay such fees to expert witnesses for work undertaken by them as are authorised for payment by the Legal Services Commission. Fees payable are either determined by the Legal Services Commission at the conclusion of the proceedings following assessment of the Solicitors bill of costs or by the Court following a detailed assessment of the Solicitors bill of costs in High Court and county court cases.

The Community Legal Service Scheme contains provision which allow Solicitors to claim payments on account from the Legal Services Commission to enable fees incurred for work done by experts to be discharged before the proceedings are concluded.

COSTS IN RELATION TO WORK UNDERTAKEN BY EXPERTS

1   On delivery of instructions, [*Name of Firm*] undertakes to be responsible for payment of the expert's reasonable charges for work undertaken in accordance with those instruction subject only to any limitations as to the amount payable which might be imposed by the Legal Services Commission upon assessment of the costs, the Court under the Protocol where applicable

or by the Court upon detailed assessment of the costs at the conclusion of the proceedings.

2   The expert agrees that the determination made by either the Legal Services Commission or the Court as to the amount of the fees payable shall be final unless otherwise agreed in writing.

3   No payment will be made to an expert unless a fee note or account has been rendered which sets out specific details of the work which has been undertaken and the time spent indicating (if appropriate) charging rates for different levels of activity undertaken.

4   Upon receipt of a fee note, [*Name of Firm*] will seek to obtain a payment on account from the Legal Services Commission to enable a proportion of not more than 75% of the expert's fees to be paid. Normally, payment will be made within two months of the claim for payment on account being submitted.

5   In the event that costs are assessed at a level below any payment made on account the expert will reimburse the difference to this Firm within 14 days of being notified by us of the outcome of the assessment.

GENERAL REQUIREMENTS OF EXPERT WITNESSES

As the Children Act jurisdiction has developed, the courts have clarified and laid down their expectations as to how expert witnesses should fulfil their obligations were instructed. Briefly stated, the primary obligations are:

1   Any report commissioned will be completed and filed within the timescale laid down by the Court.

2   Opinions should only be expressed if genuinely held and are based on all the material facts and documentation available and have been properly researched.

3   All information and documentation seen and considered, together with any research material, information or documentation referred to should be detailed in the report prepared by the expert.

4   Any report prepared by the expert will be filed with the court and disclosed to all parties and other experts instructed in the case.

5   If a number of experts in the same field are instructed, they will be required to hold discussions with the other experts and to set out, in writing, prior to trial areas of agreement and dispute between them and each expert should normally give an opinion upon each set of competing facts.

SOLICITOR'S OBLIGATIONS

As Franchise holders, [*Name of Firm*] require any expert instructed by them to be able to comply with the above. To facilitate the work to be undertaken by an expert, [*Name of Firm*] will ensure that any instructions delivered will comply with the following:

1   The expert's availability, and willingness, to accept instructions will have been checked with the expert as will the timescale within which a report can be completed.

2   The schedule of the proposed work, and the estimated fees, will have been discussed and agreed subject to any limitations imposed by the Legal Services Commission or the courts.

3   A detailed letter of instruction will be provided giving a synopsis of the proceedings, identifying issues which are agreed and disputed and identifying the issues on which opinion is sought including any specific questions which may require to be answered by the expert.

4   The instructions will be accompanied by a properly scheduled bundle of documents relevant to the issues which the expert is being asked to address.

5   Any further relevant information, or other experts' reports obtained prior to trial, will be supplied to the expert for consideration and a request made for a further addendum report, if necessary.

6   Efforts will be made to try and ensure that attendance at experts' meetings, or at the Court to give evidence, will be arranged to suit the expert's convenience and, where possible, the expert's availability will be checked before listing the case for trial.

7   If information is subsequently received that an expert's attendance at a trial is not going to be required, then the expert will be informed as soon as conveniently possible.

8   [*Name of Firm*] will endeavour to discharge the expert's fees as soon as possible after receipt of an invoice or account subject to the provisos set out above.

9   [*Name of Firm*] will endeavour to ensure that the expert is provided promptly with the result of the case in which the expert has been involved including specific feedback on their work if any was given.

Appendix 9

COURTS HEARING FAMILY CASES

1 Cases under the Children Act are heard at every level of court within the Family Justice System and the objective, in due course, is to create an integrated family court. Public law cases, where a local authority seeks a care or supervision order, must be commenced in the Family Proceedings Court (FPC), where they are heard by a bench of lay magistrates or, in some cities, by a stipendiary magistrate (now known as a District Judge (Magistrates' Court) (DJ(MC)) either sitting alone or with lay justices. However, the more serious or difficult care cases are usually transferred to the county court, where they are heard by Circuit Judges known as a 'care' judges (that is judges who have attended a special training course organised by the Judicial Studies Board (JSB)). Sometimes they are heard by Recorders (senior members of the legal profession who have also undergone special training by the JSB) or sometimes they are heard by district judges, that is professional judges of the county court ranking below the circuit bench, but who have been selected and trained to hear care cases.

2 The most difficult or serious cases are transferred up to the High Court, where they are heard by judges of the Family Division, or by senior Circuit Judges who have been given special dispensation to hear High Court cases or by Queen's Counsel sitting as Deputy High Court Judges.

3 Private law cases, that is disputes usually between parents or other family members over residence or contact or some other aspect of the exercise of parental responsibility may be commenced in any level of court and can then be transferred up or down as the seriousness or difficult of the case requires.

4 In a public law case, you may thus find yourself writing a report for or giving evidence to lay justices or a DJ(MC) in the FPC, or a Circuit Judge or Recorder or district judge in the county court or, in the High Court, a full time High Court Judge, a specially qualified Circuit Judge or Deputy High Court Judge.

5 Lay justices are unlikely to intervene and ask questions in the way that a professional DJ(MC) or Circuit Judge or High Court Judge will do so. In addition, the clerk in the FPC (now known as a legal adviser) will be a qualified lawyer, who will not only make a note of the evidence, but will advise the magistrates on any point of law or evidence which arises. You

should therefore not be surprised if the justices' clerk plays a proactive role in the proceedings.

6   The current President (Sir Mark Potter, P) is very keen to encourage lay justices to hear more cases and to sit longer than one day at a time. It is increasingly possible, therefore, that you might find yourself giving evidence in the FPC.

Appendix 10

THE CHILDREN AND FAMILIES COURT ADVISORY AND SUPPORT SERVICE (CAFCASS)

The best exposition of this subject is undoubtedly that contained in *Working in the Family Justice System*, by Elizabeth Walsh 2nd edn (Family Law, 2006) paragraphs 2.55–2.85.

CAFCASS was created on 1 April 2001 and was expected to perform the functions previously undertaken by (1) guardians ad litem in care proceedings; (2) court welfare officers in private law proceedings; and (3) the functions of the Official Solicitor relating to children. In April 2005, the functions of CAFCASS relating to Wales were devolved to the Welsh Assembly, and are now performed by CAFCASS CYMRU.

Prior to 2001, children in care proceedings were allocated a guardian ad litem, an experienced social worker who was nearly always a member of the panel of guardians ad litem and reporting officers (GALRO). Its national association was – and still is – called NAGALRO. The term 'guardian ad litem', however, has now been abandoned, and replaced by the phrase 'children's guardian'.

In care proceedings, the function of the children's guardian (now nearly always an officer of CAFCASS appointed by the court) is to safeguard the interests of the child in those proceedings. The children's guardian is given very wide powers of investigation by s 42 of the Children Act 1989, and invariably instructs a solicitor. Children in care proceedings thus have the advantage of what has become known as the 'tandem model' of representation by solicitor and guardian. One of the guardian's many functions is to protect the child he or she represents against poor social work practice.

Another important function of the children's guardian in care proceedings, and which relates directly to you, is that if expert evidence is required, the judge will frequently direct that it be obtained by the guardian on the child's behalf, or that the guardian will act as the lead solicitor in a joint instruction. Also, as explained in Chapter 13, it is frequently the guardian or the solicitor instructed by the guardian who chairs meetings of experts ordered by the court.

In private law proceedings, the CAFCASS officer is described as the Court Reporter or Court Reporting Officer (CRO). The function of the CRO is to investigate the case on the court's behalf and to make recommendations as to the course the court should adopt in the best interests of the child.

In private law proceedings, a CAFCASS Officer will also play a role in the process of in-court conciliation, designed to divert parental disputes away from contested courtroom hearings.

In adoption proceedings, if the matter is not contested, the CAFCAS Officer will simply report. In more complex or disputed cases, the CAFCASS Officer will be appointed the children's guardian and perform a similar role to that played in care proceedings.

CAFCASS also has an in-house legal department, which includes a duty officer providing advice. It also represents children in urgent medical cases – such as *Portsmouth NHS Trust v Wyatt*. In this capacity, an out of hours service is provided, and CAFCASS Legal will often instruct medical specialists to advise on the treatment / refusal of treatment issue. It is also the first port of call if separate representation is required in a difficult private law case, and where a particular point of law arises, will provide an advocate to the court (previously known as an *amicus curiae*).

You are most likely to come across CAFCASS Officers when they are acting as guardians for children in care proceedings. As may be imagined, they provide key services across the Family Justice System, and the role of CAFCASS is perceived by most practitioners as both expanding and essential to its proper functioning.

You can access the CAFCASS website at www.cafcass.gov.uk.

Appendix 11

PROPOSED GUIDANCE ON EXPERT AND ASSESSORS IN PROCEEDINGS RELATING TO CHILDREN

What follows is the draft of parts of the proposed Practice Direction in relation to expert evidence in proceedings relating to children which, when promulgated, will supersede Appendix C to the Public Law Protocol. It is also intended that the Protocol itself will be replaced by the Public Law Outline.

The author and the publishers are extremely grateful to the President of the Family Division, the authors of the proposed Practice Direction and the Ministry of Justice for making the draft of the Practice Direction available and for giving their permission for it to be published in this Appendix in draft form. It needs to be emphasised that what follows is a draft, and should be treated as such until the Practice Direction is issued in its final form.

It is reproduced here in order to enable expert witnesses to have a proper understanding of the current thinking of the Department, the Judiciary and Practitioners in relation to expert evidence in Family Proceedings relating to children. Readers of this draft should, however, be aware that although here presented in its latest form, it is susceptible to further amendment.

In the interests of space, section 8 of the Practice Direction, which deals with the appointment of assessors (who are usually only appointed in relation to disputes over costs) has been omitted, as has the Annex relating to questions to be posed to experts proposed by the Family Justice Council, and which are already to be found in Appendix 2.

Particular note should be taken of the passages in italics, which represent either changes to the matters contained in Appendix C to the Protocol or places where the wording of the Practice Direction has to be finalised. Passages from the draft which have been omitted as being either purely formal or not of direct relevance for present purposes are illustrated by a series of dots (...).

Attention is drawn in particular to the narrative introduction contained in section 1 and to the General Matters set out in section 2, which set out the thinking underlying the Practice Direction and the approach of the courts to expert evidence.

1.   INTRODUCTION

1.1   Sections 1 to 7 of this Practice Direction deal with the use of expert evidence and the instruction of experts in public-law Children Act proceedings [family proceedings relating to children]…

Where the guidance refers to 'an expert' or 'the expert', this includes a reference to an or the expert team.

Objective of the guidance on experts and expert evidence

1.2   The guidance in sections 1 to 7 aims to provide the court in public law Children Act proceedings [family proceedings relating to children] with early information to determine whether an expert, or expert evidence, will assist the court to:

- identify, narrow and where possible agree the issues between the parties;
- provide an opinion about a question that is not within the skill and experience of the court;
- encourage the early identification of questions that need to be answered by an expert; and
- encourage disclosure of full and frank information between the parties, the court and any expert instructed.

1.3   The guidance does not aim to cover all possible eventualities. Thus it should be complied with so far as is, in all the circumstances, consistent with the just disposal of the matter in accordance [with the overriding objective and] with the rules/guidance applying to the procedure in question.

Permission to instruct an expert or to use expert evidence

1.4   What the court's permission is required for varies according to the type of family proceeding:

- the general rule … is that the court's permission is required to call an expert or to put in evidence an expert's report;
- an additional principle, applying only to proceedings relating to children, is that the court's permission is required to instruct an expert: see paragraphs 1.5 to 1.8.

For the purposes of this guidance, 'proceedings relating to children' are:

(1) placement and adoption proceedings, and
(2) family proceedings held in private which (a) relate to the exercise of the inherent jurisdiction of the High Court with respect to children, (b) are brought under the Children Act 1989 in any family court, or (c) are brought in the High Court and county courts and 'otherwise relate wholly or mainly to the maintenance or upbringing of a minor'.

The phrase 'proceedings relating to children' is a convenient description: it is not a legal term of art and has no statutory force.

1.5 Proceedings relating to children are confidential and, in the absence of the court's permission, disclosure of information and documents relating to such proceedings risks contravening the law of contempt of court and/or the various statutory provisions protecting this confidentiality. Thus, under FPR 1991, rule 10.20A(2)(vii) [and FPAR 2005 rule 78(1)(c)(vii)], for the purposes of the law of contempt of court, information relating to such proceedings (whether or not contained in a document filed with the court / recorded in any form) may be communicated only to an expert whose instruction by a party has been permitted by the court. Additionally, in proceedings under the Children Act 1989, the court's permission is required to cause the child to be medically or psychiatrically examined or otherwise assessed for the purpose of the preparation of expert evidence for use in the proceedings; and, where the court's permission has not been given, no evidence arising out of such an examination or assessment may be adduced without the court's permission: FPR 1991, rule 4.18(1) and (3).

1.6 In practice, the need to have the court's permission to disclose information or documents to an expert – and, in Children Act 1989 proceedings, to have the child examined or assessed – means that in proceedings relating to children the court strictly controls the number, fields of expertise and identity of the experts who may be first instructed and then called.

1.7 Before permission is obtained from the court to instruct an expert in proceedings relating to children, it will plainly be necessary for the party wishing to instruct an expert to make enquiries designed to place before the court the information about the expert concerned which will enable the court to make the decision about whether or not permission should be given for the expert to be instructed. In practice, enquiries may need to be made of more than one expert for this purpose. This will in turn require the expert or experts concerned to be given sufficient information about the case to enable the expert to decide whether or not he or she is in a position to accept instructions. Such preliminary enquiries and the disclosure of anonymised information about the case which is a necessary part of such enquiries will not require the court's permission and will not amount to a contempt of court: see section 4A.1 and 4A.2 (Preliminary Enquiries of the Expert and Expert's Response to Preliminary Enquiries).

1.8 Section 4A gives guidance on applying for the court's permission to instruct an expert, and instructing the expert, in proceedings relating to children. The court, when granting permission to instruct an expert, will also give directions for the expert to be called to give evidence, or for the expert's report to be put in evidence: see section 4A.4 (Draft Order for the relevant hearing).

[…]

When should the court be asked for permission?

1.9   The key event is 'the relevant hearing' which is any hearing at which the court's permission to instruct an expert and/or to use expert evidence is sought. Expert issues should be raised with the court – and, where appropriate, with the other parties – as early as possible. This means:

*   in public-law Children-Act 1989 proceedings, by/at the Case Management Conference: see the Public Law Outline, paragraph(s):
*   in private-law Children-Act 1989 proceedings, by/at the First Hearing Dispute Resolution Appointment: see the Private Law Programme (9th November 2004), section 4 (Process);
*   in placement and adoption proceedings, by/at the First Directions Hearing: see FPAR 2005 rule 26 and the President's Guidance: Adoption: the New Law and Procedure (March 2006), paragraph 23.]

[...]

2.   GENERAL MATTERS

Scope of the Guidance

2.1   Sections 1 to 7 of this guidance apply to any steps taken for the purpose of public law Children Act proceedings [family proceedings relating to children] by experts (whether acting as individual experts or as members of an expert team), or those who instruct them, on or after [October 2007].

The Public Law Outline and this guidance do not apply to cases issued before [*October 2007*], but the court may direct in any individual case that *the Public Law Outline* and this guidance will apply, either wholly or partly. This subject to the overriding objective for the type of proceedings, and to the proviso that such a direction will neither cause further delay nor involve repetition of steps already taken or decisions already made in the case.

2.2   Sections 1 to 7 apply to all experts who *[...]* are or have been instructed to give or prepare evidence for the purpose of family proceedings *relating to children* in a court in England and Wales *[...]*.

2.3   [*Relates to section 8 and has been omitted*]

Pre-application instruction of experts

2.4   When experts' reports are commissioned before the commencement of proceedings, it should be made clear to the expert that they may in due course be reporting to the court and should therefore consider themselves bound by this guidance *[...]*. A prospective party to public law Children Act proceedings [family proceedings relating to children], eg a local authority, should always write a letter of instruction when asking a potential witness for a report or an opinion, whether that request is within proceedings or pre-proceedings, e.g., when commissioning specialist assessment materials, reports from a treating expert or other evidential materials and the letter of instruction should conform to the principles set out in this guidance.

Emergency and urgent cases

2.5 In emergency or urgent cases (e.g., where, before formal issue of proceedings, a without-notice application is made to the court during or out of business hours; or where, after proceedings have been issued, a previously unforeseen need for (further) expert evidence arises at short notice), a party may wish to call expert evidence without having complied with all or any part of this *guidance*. In such circumstances, the party wishing to call the expert evidence must apply forthwith to the court – where possible or appropriate, on notice to the other parties – for directions to as the future steps to be taken in respect of the expert evidence in question.

Orders

2.6 Where an order or direction requires an act to be done by an expert, or otherwise affects an expert, the party instructing that expert – or, in the case of a jointly instructed expert, the lead solicitor – must serve a copy of the order/direction on the expert forthwith on receipt of the order.

3. THE DUTIES OF EXPERTS

Overriding Duty

3.1 An expert in family proceedings *relating to children* has an overriding duty to the court that takes precedence over any obligation to the person from whom he has received instructions or by whom he is paid.

Particular Duties

3.2 Among any other duties an expert may have, an expert shall have regard to the following duties:

- to assist the court in accordance with the overriding duty;
- to provide advice to the court that conforms to the best practice of the expert's professional training;
- to provide an opinion that is independent of the party or parties instructing the expert;
- to confine the opinion to matters material to the issues between the parties and in relation only to questions that are within the expert's expertise (skill and experience). If a question is put which falls outside that expertise, *at*

the earliest possible stage the expert must say so *and should volunteer an opinion as to whether another expert is required to bring expertise not possessed by those already involved or, in the rare case, whether a second opinion is required on a key issue and, if possible, what question(s) should be asked of the second expert;*
- in expressing an opinion, to take into consideration all of the material facts including any relevant factors arising from ethnic, cultural, religious or linguistic contexts at the time the opinion is expressed;
- to inform those instructing the expert without delay of any change in the opinion and the reason for the change.

Content of the Expert's Report

3.3   The expert's report shall be addressed to the court *and prepared and filed in accordance with the court's timetable* and shall:

- give details of the expert's qualifications and experience;
- contain a statement setting out the substance of all material instructions (whether written or oral) summarising the facts stated and instructions given to the expert which are material to the conclusions and opinions expressed in the report;
- identify materials that have not been produced either as original medical (or other professional) records or in response to an instruction from a party, as such materials may contain an assumption as to the standard of proof, the admissibility or otherwise of hearsay evidence, and other important procedural and substantive questions relating to the different purposes of other enquiries (e.g., criminal or disciplinary proceedings);
- identify all requests to third parties for disclosure and their responses, to avoid partial disclosure, which tends only to prove a case rather than give full and frank information;
- make clear which of the facts stated in the report are within the expert's own knowledge;
- state who carried out any test, examination or interview which the expert has used for the report and whether or not the test, examination or interview has been carried out under the expert's supervision;
- give details of the qualifications of any person who carried out the test, examination or interview;

in expressing an opinion to the court:
- take into consideration all of the material facts including any relevant factors arising from ethnic, cultural, religious or linguistic contexts at the time the opinion is expressed, identifying the facts, literature and any other material (including research material) that the expert has relied upon in forming an opinion;
- describe their own professional risk assessment process and/or process of differential diagnosis, highlighting factual assumptions, deductions from the

factual assumptions, and any unusual, contradictory or inconsistent features of the case;

- highlight whether a proposition is an hypothesis (in particular a controversial hypothesis), or an opinion deduced in accordance with peer reviewed and tested technique, research and experience accepted as a consensus in the scientific community;
- indicate whether the opinion is provisional (or qualified, as the case may be), stating the qualification and the reason for it, and identifying what further information is required to give an opinion without qualification;

where there is a range of opinion on any question to be answered by the expert:
- summarise the range of opinion;
- highlight and analyse within the range of opinion an 'unknown cause', whether on the facts of the case (eg there is too little information to form a scientific opinion) or because of limited experience, lack of research, peer review or support in the field of expertise which the expert professes;
- give reasons for any opinion expressed: the use of a balance sheet approach to the factors that support or undermine an opinion can be of great assistance to the court;
- contain a summary of the expert's conclusions and opinions;
- contain a statement that the expert understands his duty to the court and has complied and will continue to comply with that duty;
- contain an additional statement that:
  - (i) the expert has no conflict of interest of any kind, other than any which he has disclosed in his report;
  - (ii) he does not consider that any interest which he has disclosed affects his suitability as an expert witness on any issue on which *he has given evidence*;
  - (iii) he will advise the party by whom he is instructed if, between the date of his report and the final hearing, there is any change in circumstances which affects his answers to (a) or (b) above;
- be verified by a statement of truth in the following form:

  'I confirm that insofar as the facts stated in my report are within my own knowledge I have made clear which they are and I believe them to be true, and that the opinions I have expressed represent my true and complete professional opinion.'

Attention is drawn to [RSC Order , rule] which sets out the consequences of verifying a document containing a false statement without an honest belief in its truth.

4A.   PREPARATION FOR THE RELEVANT HEARING

Preliminary Enquiries of the Expert

4A.1   In time for the information requested to be available before the advocates' meeting which takes place before the relevant hearing, the solicitor for the party proposing to instruct the expert (or lead solicitor/solicitor for the child if the instruction proposed is joint) shall approach the expert with the following information:

- the nature of the proceedings and the issues likely to require determination by the court;
- the questions about which the expert is to be asked to give an opinion (including any ethnic, cultural, religious or linguistic contexts);
- when the court is to be asked to give permission for the instruction (if
- unusually permission has already been given, the date and details of that permission);
- whether permission is asked of the court for the instruction of another expert in the same or any related field (i.e. to give an opinion on the same or related questions);
- the volume of reading which the expert will need to undertake;
- whether or not (in an appropriate case) permission has been applied for or given for the expert to examine the child;
- whether or not (in an appropriate case) it will be necessary for the expert to conduct interviews (and, if so, with whom);
- the likely timetable of legal and social work steps;
- when the expert's opinion is likely to be required;
- whether and, if so, what date has been fixed by the court for any hearing at which the expert may be required to give evidence (in particular the Final Hearing).

It is essential that there should be proper co-ordination between the court and the expert when drawing up the case management timetable: the needs of the court should be balanced with the needs of the expert (or expert team), whose forensic work is undertaken as an adjunct to his, her or their main professional duties, whether in the National Health Service or elsewhere.

The expert should be informed at this stage of initial contact that he/she (or in the case of an expert team, they) may, through their instructing solicitor, make representations to the court about being named or otherwise identified in any public judgment given by the court.

Expert's Response to Preliminary Enquiries

4A.2   In time for the advocates' meeting before the relevant hearing, the solicitors intending to instruct the expert shall obtain the following information from the expert:

- that acceptance of the proposed instructions will not involve the expert in any conflict of interest;
- that the work required is within the expert's expertise;
- that the expert is available to do the relevant work within the suggested time scale;
- when the expert is available to give evidence, the dates and/or times to avoid, and, where a hearing date has not been fixed, the amount of notice the expert will require to make arrangements to come to court (or to give evidence by video link) without undue disruption to their normal professional routines;
- the cost, including hourly or other charging rates, and likely hours to be spent, of attending experts' meetings, attending court and writing the report (to include any examinations and interviews);
- any representations which the expert wishes to make to the court about being named or otherwise identified in any public judgment given by the court.

Where parties have not agreed on the appointment of a single joint expert before the relevant hearing, they should obtain the above confirmations in respect of all

experts they intend to put to the court for the purpose of [RSC Order , rule].

The proposal to instruct an expert

4A.3 Any party who proposes to ask the court for permission to instruct an expert shall, **by 11 a.m. on the day before the case management hearing or other relevant hearing**, file and serve a written proposal to instruct the expert in the following detail:

- the name, discipline, qualifications and expertise of the expert (by way of C.V. where possible);
- the expert's availability to undertake the work;
- the relevance of the expert evidence sought to be adduced to the issues in the proceedings and the specific questions upon which it is proposed the expert should give an opinion (including the relevance of any ethnic, cultural, religious or linguistic contexts);
- the timetable for the report;
- the responsibility for instruction;
- whether or not the expert evidence can properly be obtained by the joint instruction of the expert by two or more of the parties;
- whether the expert evidence can properly be obtained by only one party (e.g., on behalf of the child);
- why the expert evidence proposed cannot be given by social services undertaking a core assessment or by the Guardian in accordance with their respective statutory duties;

- the likely cost of the report on an hourly or other charging basis: where possible, the expert's terms of instruction should be made available to the court;
- the proposed apportionment (at least in the first instance) of any jointly instructed expert's fee; when it is to be paid; and, if applicable, whether public funding has been approved.

Draft Order for the relevant hearing

4A.4   Any party proposing to instruct an expert shall in the draft order submitted **in preparation (i.e., not less than 2 days before) for the relevant hearing** request the court to give directions (among any others) as to the following:

- the party who is to be responsible for drafting the letter of instruction and providing the documents to the expert;
- the issues identified by the court and the questions about which the expert is to give an opinion;
- the timetable within which the report is to be prepared, filed and served;
    4) the disclosure of the report to the parties and to any other expert;
    5) the organisation of, preparation for and conduct of an experts' discussion;
    6) the preparation of a statement of agreement and disagreement by the experts following an experts' discussion;
    7) making available to the judge at an early opportunity the expert reports in electronic form;
    8) the attendance of the expert at the Final Hearing (or to give evidence for that hearing by alternative means, e.g., in writing or by video link); unless agreement is reached at or before the Pre-Hearing Review ("PHR") c:– or, if no PHR is to be held, by a specified date prior to the Final Hearing – about the opinions given by the expert.

4B.   Letter of Instruction

4B.1   The solicitor instructing the expert shall, **within 5 days after the relevant hearing**, prepare (agree with the other parties where appropriate) file and serve a letter of instruction to the expert which shall:

- set out the context in which the expert's opinion is sought (including any ethnic, cultural, religious or linguistic contexts);
- define carefully the specific questions the expert is required to answer, ensuring:
    - that they are within the ambit of the expert's area of expertise; and
    - that they do not contain unnecessary or irrelevant detail;
    - that the questions addressed to the expert are kept to a manageable number and are clear, focused and direct;

- that the questions reflect what the expert has been requested to do by the court;
- the Annex to this guidance sets out suggested questions in letters of instruction (1) to child mental health professionals or paediatricians, and (2) adult psychiatrists and adult psychologists, in Children Act 1989 proceedings [proceedings relating to children?];
- list the documentation provided, or provide for the expert an indexed and paginated bundle which shall include:
  - a copy of the order (or those parts of the order) which gives permission for the instruction of the expert, immediately the order becomes available;
  - an agreed list of essential reading;
  - all new documentation when it is filed and regular updates to the list of documents provided, or to the index to the paginated bundle;
  - a copy of this guidance;
- identify materials that have not been produced either as original medical (or other professional) records or in response to an instruction from a party, as such materials may contain an assumption as to the standard of proof, the admissibility or otherwise of hearsay evidence, and other important procedural and substantive questions relating to the different purposes of other enquiries (eg criminal or disciplinary proceedings);
- identify all requests to third parties for disclosure and their responses, to avoid partial disclosure, which tends only to prove a case rather than give full and frank information;
- identify the relevant lay and professional people concerned with the proceedings (e.g., the treating clinicians) and inform the expert of his/her right to talk to the other professionals provided an accurate record is made of the discussion(s);
- identify any other expert instructed in the proceedings and advise the expert of his/her right to talk to the other experts provided an accurate record is made of the discussion;
- define the contractual basis upon which the expert is retained and in particular the funding mechanism including how much the expert will be paid (an hourly rate and overall estimate should already have been obtained), when the expert will be paid, and what limitation there might be on the amount the expert can charge for the work which he/she will have to do. In cases where the parties are publicly funded, there should also be a brief explanation of the detailed assessment process;
- where the court has directed that the instructions to the expert are to be contained in a jointly agreed letter, any instructing party may submit to the court a written request, which must be copied to the other instructing parties, that the court settle the letter of instruction. Where possible, the written request should be set out in an e-mail to the court, preferably sent directly

to the judge dealing with the proceedings (or, in the Family Proceedings Court, to the legal adviser who will forward it to the appropriate judge or justice(s)), and copied by e-mail to the other instructing parties. The court will settle the letter of instruction, usually – in order to avoid delay – without a hearing; and will send (where practicable, by e-mail) the settled letter to the lead solicitor for transmission forthwith to the expert, and copy it to the other instructing parties for information.

4C.   THE COURT'S CONTROL OF EXPERT EVIDENCE: CONSEQUENTIAL ISSUES

Written Questions

4C.1   Any party wishing to put written questions to an expert or SJE for the purpose of clarifying the expert's report must put the questions to the expert or SJE **not later than 10 days after receipt of the report**.

The court will specify the timetable according to which the expert or SJE is to answer the written questions.

Experts' Discussion/Meeting: Purpose

4C.2   By 'the specified date' (a specified date prior to the hearing at which the expert is to give oral evidence) – or, if a PHR is to be held, by the PHR – the court may give directions for the experts to meet or communicate:

- to identify and narrow the issues in the case;
- where possible, to reach agreement on the expert questions;
- to identify the reasons for disagreement on any expert question and what if any action needs to be taken to resolve any outstanding disagreement / question;
- to obtain elucidation or amplification of relevant evidence in order to assist the court to determine the issues;
- to limit, wherever possible, the need for experts to attend court to give oral evidence.

Experts' Discussion/Meeting: Arrangements

4C.3   In accordance with the directions given by the court, the solicitor or other professional who is given the responsibility by the court ('the nominated professional') shall - within 10 days after the experts' reports have been filed – make arrangements for the experts to meet or communicate. Where applicable, the following matters should be considered:

- where permission has been given for the instruction of experts from different disciplines, a global discussion may be held relating to those questions that concern all or most of them;

- separate discussions may have to be held among experts from the same or related disciplines, but care should be taken to ensure that the discussions complement each other so that related questions are discussed by all relevant experts;

- 7 days prior to a discussion or meeting, the nominated professional should formulate an agenda including a list of […] questions for consideration. The agenda should contain only those questions which are intended to clarify areas of agreement or disagreement. Questions which repeat questions asked in the letter of instruction and/or which seek to rehearse cross-examination in advance of the hearing should be rejected as likely to defeat the purpose of the meeting;

- the agenda may usefully take the form of a list of questions to be circulated among the other parties in advance. The agenda should comprise all questions that each party wishes the experts to consider. The agenda and list of questions should be sent to each of the experts not later than 2 days before the discussion;

- the nominated professional may exercise his or her discretion to accept further questions after the agenda with list of questions has been circulated to the parties. **Only in exceptional circumstances should questions be added to the agenda within the 2-day period before the meeting. Under no circumstances should any question received on the day of, or during, the meeting, be accepted.** Strictness in this regard is vital, for adequate notice of the questions enables the parties to identify and isolate the issues in the case before the meeting so that the experts' discussion at the meeting can concentrate on those issues;

5) the discussion should usually be chaired by the nominated professional – or, in exceptional cases, where the parties have applied to the court – by an independent professional identified by the parties or the court. In complex cases, it may be necessary for the discussion to be jointly chaired by this professional and an expert. A minute must be taken of the questions answered by the experts, and a Statement of Agreement and Disagreement must be prepared which should be agreed and signed by each of the experts who participated in the discussion. The statement should be served and filed **not later than 5 days after the discussion has taken place;**

6) consideration should be given in each case to whether some or all of the experts participate by telephone conference or video link to ensure that minimum disruption is caused to professional schedules and to minimise costs.

Meetings/conferences attended by a single joint expert ('SJE')

4C.4   SJEs should not attend any meeting or conference which is not a joint one, unless all the parties have agreed in writing or the court has directed that such a meeting may be held, and it is agreed or directed who is to pay the expert's fees for the meeting/conference. Any meeting/conference attended by an SJE should be proportionate to the case.

Court-directed meetings involving experts in public-law Children Act cases

4C.5   In public-law Children Act proceedings, where the court gives a direction that a meeting shall take place between the local authority and any relevant named experts for the purpose of providing assistance to the local authority in the formulation of plans and proposals for the child, the meeting shall be arranged, chaired and minuted in accordance with the directions given by the court.

5.   POSITIONS OF THE PARTIES

5.1   Where *a* party refuses to be bound by an agreement that has been reached at an experts' discussion/meeting, that party must inform the court by letter filed at the court and copied to the other parties **within 10 days after the discussion/meeting (or, where a PHR is to be held, not less than 5 days before the PHR)** of his reasons for refusing to accept the agreement.

6.   ARRANGING FOR THE EXPERT TO *GIVE EVIDENCE*

Preparation

6.1   Where the court has directed the attendance of an expert witness, the party who is responsible for the instruction of the expert shall ensure **by the specified date (or the PHR):**

*   that a date and time (if possible, convenient to the expert) are fixed for the court to hear the expert's evidence, and that this fixture is made substantially in advance of the hearing at which the expert is to give oral evidence and no later than a specified date prior to that hearing or, where a PHR is to be held, than the PHR;
*   that, if the expert's oral evidence is not required, the expert is notified as soon as possible;
*   that the witness template accurately indicates how long the expert is likely to be giving evidence, in order to avoid the inconvenience of the expert being delayed at court;
4)   that consideration is given in each case to whether some or all of the experts participate by telephone conference or video link, *or submit their evidence in writing,* to ensure that minimum disruption is caused to professional schedules and to minimise costs.

Expert(s) attending Court

6.2   Where expert witnesses are to be called, all parties shall ensure, by the specified date (or, where a PHR is to be held, by the PHR)**, that:**

- the parties' advocates have identified (whether at an advocates' meeting or by other means) the issues which the experts are to address;
- wherever possible, a logical sequence to the evidence is arranged, with experts of the same discipline giving evidence on the same day(s);
- [...] the court is informed of any circumstance where all experts agree but a party nevertheless does not accept the agreed opinion, so that directions can be given for the proper consideration of the experts' evidence and the parties' reasons for not accepting the same;
- in the exceptional case the court is informed of the need for a witness summons.

7.   ACTION AFTER THE *FINAL* HEARING

7.1   Within 10 days after the Final Hearing, **the (lead) solicitor instructing the expert** *shall* **provide feedback to the expert by way of a letter informing the expert of the outcome of the case, and the use made by the court of the expert's opinion.**

7.2   Where the court directs preparation of a transcript, it may direct that the (lead) solicitor instructing the expert *shall* send a copy to the **expert within 10 days after receiving the transcript.**

7.3   After a Final Hearing in the Family Proceedings Court, the (lead) solicitor instructing the expert shall send a copy of the court's written reasons for its decision to the expert **within 10 days after receiving the written reasons**.

INDEX